AF566613

LEVERAGING web SERVICES

LEVERAGING WEB SERVICES

Planning, Building, and Integration for Maximum Impact

John Edwards

BPI INDIA PVT LTD

BPI INDIA PVT LTD

F-213/A, Ground Floor, Old Mehrauli Badarpur Road,
Lado Sarai, New Delhi- 110030 (India)
Tel: +91-11-43394300-99
e-mail: sales@bpiindia.com

ISBN : 978818497537-6

Published by: BPI INDIA PVT LTD, 2012

Printed and bound in India

To my family, particularly Sandie Keiser, who kept me nourished with delicious chocolates throughout the writing of this book

Contents

Acknowledgment

The author wishes to recognize the untiring efforts of Eve Keiser in the creation of this book. Her endless hours of research and coordination are reflected on every page.

Introduction

Why Web Services?

On March 10, 2000, the NASDAQ Composite Index topped out at 5,047. Three years later, on March 10, 2003, the index closed at 1,278. Somewhere between those two dates the high-tech bubble had burst and a new, more frugal era in information technology (IT) had begun. With the unrealistic hopes of "The New Economy" fading away, many promising technologies were suddenly "out." Cost cutting and retrenchment spread across the IT landscape.

At around this same time, a new technology known as Web services began moving to the forefront of the IT environment. Unlike many other Internet-oriented enterprise tools, which gained overnight popularity and vanished almost as quickly, Web services have defied the odds and remain a significant and rapidly growing technology.

Web services, in a nutshell, are Web-based applications that dynamically interact with other Web applications using open standards. Web services aren't revolutionary, but their standards-based approach to integration and interoperability makes them a contender for "next big thing" status.

Unlike earlier component-oriented software, Web services are founded on widely accepted industry standards. Web services utilize Extensible Markup Language (XML)–based standards. Extensible Markup Language is an open standard for data description that's used to define data elements on a Web page and in business-to-business documents. Extensible Markup Language and related standards, such as Simple Object Access Protocol (SOAP), Universal Description, Discovery, and Integration (UDDI), and Web Services Description Language (WSDL), allow applications to communicate with each other over the Internet. Besides these standards, more complex Web services rely on numerous other specifications to facilitate collaboration among trading partners.

What Are Web Services?

The simplest way to view Web services is as software that knows how to talk to other types of software over a network. A Web service can be nearly any type of application that has the ability to define to other applications what it does, and it can perform that action for authorized applications or parties. Web services are essentially an infrastructure layer between existing component models. Specifically, a Web service fits the following criteria:

- It is able to expose and describe itself to other applications, allowing those applications to understand what the service does.
- It can be located by other applications via an online directory, if the service has been registered in the directory.
- It can be invoked by the originating application by using standard protocols.

Web services allow organizations to use applications in new and innovative ways. An airline, for example, might use Web services technology to mesh its mainframe-based reservations database to Linux server-based reservation systems operated by hotels and car rental companies. To do this type of integration in the past, one had to build custom connectors between these applications. With Web services, the work is basically accomplished with XML.

A simple Web service is characterized by the three standards—SOAP, UDDI, and WSDL—which, taken together, provide a basic "request and response" functionality. Simple Web services usually are not transactional in nature. Instead, they generate a general request for information. Simple Web services can be used to efficiently deliver information such as news, stock, and weather reports to Web sites.

On the other hand, a complex Web service might involve multiparty, long-running transactions with several trading partners or suppliers. If a retailer needs to stock up on Christmas toys, for example, it could use a Web services application to send a request for proposal via the Internet. Design suppliers could automatically respond to the request and send their offer to an online marketplace. Then, the originating application could automatically select the most cost-effective offer.

Another example of a complex Web service is the ability of a supplier to query an enterprise database in order to anticipate a customer's needs. Imagine that an automaker has a database with inventory information and access to 1,000 suppliers. It would be beneficial if those suppliers could request information, directly from the automaker's database, on the inventory level of the parts they supply. If the inventory falls below a predetermined level, the software could automatically trigger a shipment of new chrome-plated wing nuts from the supplier to the automaker, for instance.

A Divided Camp

The Web services field is split into two camps. On one side, Microsoft is promoting .NET, a Web services initiative that requires the use of Windows-based software. Sun Microsystems, on the other hand, is spearheading a Java-oriented Web services strategy. While Microsoft has the advantage of being the world's largest software company, Sun has the benefit of a more open and flexible strategy. Supported by more than thirty major vendors, Sun's Java 2 Platform, Enterprise Edition (J2EE) is the fulfillment of a services-driven network vision that Sun has held for several years, resulting in Java, Jini, and similar sophisticated technologies.

The strength of J2EE lies in the fact that it doesn't bind users to a single company's vision. It is built on things that have been around for a while, whereas .NET is a rearchitecture of the Microsoft platform. As a result, .NET tends to appeal most to organizations that are already deeply committed to Windows.

Microsoft's track record on embracing open standards is also contributing to a sense of uneasiness about .NET. The software giant has a long history of latching onto open standards only to add proprietary extensions that are tailored toward its own servers and clients. Will XML and SOAP fare any better in Microsoft's hands than, say, Java? At this point, nobody really knows.

Strength in Web Services

Web services are marked by their independent natures. Their strength lies in this independence. It doesn't matter if linking organizations are using a mainframe versus a Windows-based NT server, or internally developed versus packaged software. Web services are platform-neutral, and adopters don't have to worry about things like binary compatibility between various operating systems.

Such neutrality is critical when it comes to integrating systems with partners. Integrating business processes between enterprises with traditional middleware has been difficult, because it's unlikely that two firms will use the same technologies. There's also a very low chance they'll be written in the same language, such as C, C++, or Java. But XML can be interpreted by any language and can be sent from any middleware, so it doesn't matter if you're using Java, Microsoft, CORBA, or whatever.

Operational simplicity is another reason a growing number of organizations are looking at Web services. With its value-defining tags, XML lets a Web services application make a remote procedure call (RPC) into a data store. That makes the exchange of even detailed information simple and almost foolproof.

Standards and simplicity lead to speedier application development at lower costs. With standards, IT managers know what they're dealing with when they develop applications—there's no mystery. Also, with standards-based development tools, vendors will no longer be able to command top dollar for use of their proprietary technologies. Additionally, Web services can improve efficiency by allowing enterprises to streamline business processes, such as supply chains between companies and their trading partners.

The technology's promise of steady work and its relatively shallow learning curve have already inspired many developers to begin acquiring Web services skills. Since learning Web services development isn't nearly as difficult as, say, switching from C++ to Java, the ability to find the talent isn't nearly as much of a problem as it has been in other new technology areas.

Web services also have the potential to provide significant cost savings. A link between two applications that don't use Web services can cost upward of $1 million. Organizations need to compare that number to the expense of retraining their developers in Web services technologies. Then, they should look at the cost of converting existing applications into Web services. The payoff will come over time for most organizations, as disparate applications are combined into a handful of Web services. Now, for example, they can build one database that's able to understand SOAP messages and communicate with thousands of people.

No Silver Bullet

In this book we'll see how Web services are beginning to affect the IT landscape. Early adopters have already implemented their first Web service projects, and the results are generally highly encouraging. Adopters are learning that Web services, when done right, can dramatically ease business-to-business (B2B) integration and speed application development.

In the upcoming chapters, we'll see how various enterprises came to believe in Web services. We'll look at how they strived to get an unproven technology past a series of business and technological hurdles. Through descriptions, war stories, anecdotes, and even a few recalled nightmares, we'll discover how IT leaders at major enterprises came to harness a powerful new business technology that promises to affect virtually every business in the world, from mom-and-pop shops to global conglomerates.

Web services certainly don't provide a silver bullet, or even a brass ring. But the technology is making it a lot easier for organizations to develop applications for accessing, distributing, and exchanging information.

LEVERAGING web SERVICES

Chapter 1

CIGNA—A Portal to Web Services

CIGNA is one of the largest health insurers in the United States, along with Aetna and United Healthcare. Including related businesses, such as dental plans, specialty medical management programs, and pharmacy benefits management, the Philadelphia-based company covers about 13 million health plan consumers.

In the insurance industry, Web services platforms are now allowing many companies to reinvent the way they use their sales channels, interact with customers, and market their products. CIGNA is one of the more aggressive firms in the employee benefits and insurance sectors using Web portals to improve its customer service.

CIGNA is offering its 16 million health and retirement plan customers Web-based portals utilizing Yahoo! Enterprise Solutions technology. CIGNA's use of portal technology, as opposed to a Web-generated customer service interface, gives its customers a higher degree of personalization and information. Unlike the generic customer service Web interfaces that customers are used to, the CIGNA/Yahoo! portal helps the company's health plan consumers manage their claims, see their own information, set preferences, and even order prescriptions using their myCIGNA.com portal page.

Eric Consolazio is senior vice president in charge of the CIGNA HealthCare information systems unit. Previously, Consolazio created and led CIGNA's eCommerce practice, which develops and implements corporate-wide strategy and technologies for e-enabling employee benefits. Before joining CIGNA in 1999, Consolazio was employed by accounting and consulting giant PricewaterhouseCoopers in New York, where he was responsible for systems integration and e-commerce within the firm's eastern region insurance practice. His responsibilities included practice development, architecture design, and systems implementation. Consolazio has also been a featured speaker at numerous industry events and has authored numerous white papers on e-commerce.

Consolazio believes that, while debate still rages about how Web services should be defined, the technology is rapidly evolving into a powerful business tool.

> If you ask fifteen different people what Web services are, you'll get twenty different answers, including those who like to define Web services almost on an atomic level. For a number of reasons, we don't define it that way. For us, a Web service is something that has tangible business value. If it doesn't fulfill some type of business function, then we really don't call it a Web service.

We began implementing Web services with the rollout of the consumer portal in July 2002. Prior to then, we had been building applications, primarily for consumer self-service and for what we call provider self-service—doctors—for the last few years.

The project was begun late in December of 2001, so we were able to deliver the portal within approximately seven months. But the underpinnings of that portal were built on applications we had been building for the last two years.

For Consolazio, Web services offer the promise of a simplified way to handle a variety of different kinds of portal users: physicians, consumers, and employers.

The reason we went with Web services was that different constituents—doctors, for example—needed to see the exact same information about a health plan that the consumer himself would see. In other cases, however, they would not. In initially building self-service, we developed online "member self-service" to serve up a person's eligibility and benefits information. In certain cases, what we wanted to do was serve up that same eligibility information for the physician.

When we were developing the portal, we wanted to be able to customize and personalize it to a person's tastes. A person may, or may not, want to see her claims, but would want to see her eligibility.

We took that monolithic application and broke it up. We basically created Java-based, XML–based Web services, and broke some up into an eligibility service, a benefits service, and a claim service. We have other services, as well. We feed those, via XML, into the portal desktop. So we were able to mix and match, as it were. We were able to customize and, ultimately, personalize information by breaking these components down into more discrete business functions and feeding them, in a standard way, through XML to the desktop.

We adopted Web services out of necessity, because, without doing so, we would have had to do redundant development. We could have actually served up different information about one person to different people, which is what we didn't want to do. We didn't want a consumer to see different information than the doctor would, if they're talking about the same thing. We wanted them to see apples-to-apples, because the consumer interfaces with the doctor. We wanted to make sure they were on the same wavelength. We didn't want to give them differing information or differing details.

Consolazio's goal was to create an all-in-one information delivery environment.

We were able then to get some synergy. Instead of having three individual, discrete projects, we basically had one integrated project where we took requirements, based on constituents, and then mixed and matched the components.

That's easier wished than done, however.

There's a lot of effort that goes into building the portal, and there's a lot of effort that goes into custom

> tailoring and securing the information for each of these constituents, be they doctors, consumers, or employers. But it made our life much, much easier. We were able to use these services and not have to build interfaces over and over again to back-end systems, some of which are mainframe systems, some of which are distributed systems. We tapped into virtually dozens of different sources of information to come up with the basic portal screen for a consumer. So that makes it very easy for us, but more importantly, it makes it very easy for consumers, as well. They can size, move, add, or delete from an inventory of functions that we've given to them in the portal.

In a move designed to simplify portal development and management, and to give users access to a wider range of information options, CIGNA decided to partner with Yahoo!.

> We actually utilize Web services provided by Yahoo!. We can, through XML feeds, bring Yahoo! News, health tips, and other information into the portal in a very standardized fashion—all of it is via standard XML feeds. To the consumer, it's one desktop. In actuality, however, it's virtually constructed from many, many different locations—from legacy systems on our back-end and different third-party sources.

CIGNA was moving toward a self-service environment before the portal became part of its infrastructure. Part of Consolazio's challenge was to efficiently integrate existing applications into the new Web services–based portal.

> We built some very good Web applications. But if you wanted to find out, for example, your medical benefits, you would come to the Web page and move into an application called Medical Self-Service. But if you wanted to find out about your pharmacy benefits, you would be moved to your pharmacy page. Only then could you could look at your pharmacy benefits.
>
> It was really a collection of different stove-piped applications, which, three or four years ago, was pretty good stuff. But as we went forward, interviewed customers, found out their preferences, and did usability studies, we discovered that it was very cumbersome for them. They had to have multiple passwords, they had to drive through different applications—it really wasn't usable. And, regardless of how we tuned the look, feel, and navigation of the Web site, it didn't have all the information in one place.
>
> We implemented this portal as a framework for the existing applications, then built a second generation of applications behind it. So, in the case of the medical self-service application, while we leveraged the components behind it, it was virtually rebuilt. We decomposed it into different Web services that we set up into this portal. Now people come in and log in once. Once they log in, they can go to different pages by clicking on different tasks, without having to worry about multiple passwords. When they actually dive down into the page, a whole summary of

information is in front of them—the key information that they need at their fingertips: pharmacy information, dental information, medical information for all their CIGNA products. In addition, their retirement information is one click away.

In essence, what we wanted to be able to do was to have all the user's critical information located on one page. We wanted to have one place from which our constituents could navigate with a single click to get where they wanted to go, and be able to get summary information—the quick hits, such as their last five claims—right there, front and center.

Yahoo! PortalBuilder software lies at the heart of myCIGNA.com. Consolazio says he was attracted to the technology by its extensive supply of information content, which CIGNA could use to inform and educate portal users.

What differentiated Yahoo! was that it was able to give us a number of different services. It was able to provide content via an XML feed that fed right into the portal with no work on our part. Additionally, PortalBuilder allows users to access myCIGNA.com directly from their existing My Yahoo! page. Users can actually place a specific icon on their My Yahoo! page so that they can click through to myCIGNA .com.

Given the amount of highly sensitive personal content that resides on myCIGNA.com, security was a top priority for Consolazio and his team.

> The portal's security aspect is handled by Netegrity SiteMinder. The product is a software platform of shared services that includes single sign-on, authentication management (who you are), and entitlement management (what you are allowed to do on the site).

CIGNA is using IBM's WebSphere for application server duties.

> IBM has a whole suite of products that wrap around WebSphere. We basically use the core WebSphere product. They have lots of bells and whistles they're willing to sell to you, but we don't use a lot of them.

For its Web server, CIGNA selected Sun Microsystems.

> We utilize the Sun Solaris operating system and the directory service—iPlanet (now SunOne) Directory Server—where we keep a lot of our security information.

The system ties together in a neat bundle.

> We have WebSphere, from which we access the Web services and also drive back to the individual transaction systems. We have the portal, which pools together all the information that's fed by XML, either from the application server, or from various places across the globe. We have Netegrity on top of it, which provides the security.

In light of the fact that CIGNA assembled its portal environment from various vendors, Consolazio doesn't see a company, or group of companies, dominating the Web services market.

> We haven't seen anybody yet who's really dominated in Web services. The way we define Web services is really according to business function. We think that, until these technology vendors have functions that add business value for a specific industry, we won't see a company that really dominates. It might be that you'll see different players dominate different niches.

Consolazio says he wasn't afraid to be an early Web services adopter, although he admits that it helps to have a tech-savvy partner that's experienced in Web services integration issues to guide the design and implementation processes.

> There are a lot of things that we did, and have done, that we believe no one else has done. The partnership of Yahoo!, the personalization and customization, the use of Web services—-this is all pretty new stuff.
>
> We wanted to make sure we partnered with substantial companies. So, with Yahoo!, we were able to leverage some good collateral.
>
> I also think you can make Web services very, very complicated. The more complicated you make it, the worse it gets, relating to scale, performance, maintenance, and reliability. We could have devised very elaborate architectures to accommodate a very atomic view of what Web services are, but we decided to stick with a design architecture that was

> very straightforward, very scalable, and that dealt with very high volumes and performance.
>
> The sobering factor for us is that we literally service millions of people. Necessity drives us away from architectural purity to something that is more realistic, easily implemented, and more scalable.

Consolazio believes that Web services are best implemented in phases, rather than as radical overhauls of existing processes and environments.

> We started with our Web site and moved backward, rather than tearing our entire infrastructure apart and implementing, in one fell swoop, some gigantic vision of Web services across the enterprise.

The myCIGNA.com portal was merely a first step toward creating a Web services–driven enterprise, says Consolazio.

> We're going to start leveraging Web services across the enterprise for different purposes. Going forward, we're looking at creating different partnerships. We want to be able to provide Web services directly to employers' desktops through trusted security, so that employers can take a service from our Web site and put it on their own site. This is the sort of thing we're exploring.
>
> We're also exploring the possibility of utilizing Web services for more touchpoints. Can we, for example, utilize XML and provide interactive voice response (IVR) to our call center? Initial results coming back

> tell us it can be done, but we have a very established infrastructure already, so the cost benefit of doing that is under question. But these are the types of things we're looking at. The real question, however, is whether there's a demand for these kinds of services, as well as if they're technically feasible.

It's difficult to get a precise grasp on just how much money Web services can save an enterprise, says Consolazio.

> I will tell you, we have gained productivity, but we haven't really quantified the specific benefits for Web services. It's just an approach by which we're building business value.

On the other hand, Consolazio notes that the ability to reuse components provides a powerful incentive for using Web service.

> We're able to reuse the same components in different ways. We're able to take eligibility information, for example, and put it on a consumer's desktop, or a doctor's desktop. The key is being able to define these components so that you're able not only to reuse them, but to build them in such a way that your Web site's users can personalize and customize their experience. That's the real value of Web services. There's a big, beautiful world out there as to how these services can customize, personalize, and add value on an individual level.

A successful Web services implementation, says Consolazio, hinges on two factors: people and organization.

Put your best people on it, and have your development effort organized and mobilized. These elements are as important as the technology that you use.

Our e-commerce capability is really funneled through a singular center of excellence that serves the entire enterprise. Without that, we would have just built divisional solutions. We wouldn't have an integrated Web site, and we wouldn't be leveraging the portal or Web services the way we are.

Chapter 2

Putnam Lovell NBF Securities—Banking on Web Services

Based in San Francisco, investment bank Putnam Lovell NBF Securities focuses on the financial services industry and, as a result, has asset management, banking, insurance, investment, and brokerage firms among its clients. In addition to mergers and acquisitions advice, private placements, and public offerings, the firm offers research on more than one hundred public companies. Putnam Lovell is an affiliate of National Bank Financial, one of Canada's largest investment banks, which acquired Putnam Lovell in 2002.

Rodric R. O'Connor was Putnam Lovell NBF's chief technology officer until February 2003, when he left to take a similar post with Blum Capital Partners, L.P., a San Francisco–based investment firm. Under O'Connor's leadership, Putnam Lovell adopted a Web services strategy. To implement the plan, he tapped Salesforce.com Enterprise to handle customer relationship management (CRM) tasks, Grand Central Communication Enterprise Solution as an integration hub, BlueMatrix Research for research content creation, and Appshop for Oracle financial applications hosting.

O'Connor says he was attracted to Web services because the technology is ideally suited for Putnam Lovell's most important task—information distribution.

> Our primary business process is distributing our research to clients via e-mail. We've accomplished that by using Web services to integrate to Internet-based applications. We are using Web services to build point-to-point integration between those applications.
>
> We have a research creation application called BlueMatrix that is a native Internet application. The server application resides on an Internet server provided and managed by BlueMatrix. Equity research analysts use the system to create equity research. It has an internal database of equity data that is populated from market feeds with share price and trading volume information. It builds a database of all the equities that we produce research on. Via a Web browser, a research analyst initiates a piece of research on a specific company. The system then prepopulates the content with numerics from the database and allows the analyst to add free-form text into their research piece. There is a work flow within the application for editorial and compliance approval, to ensure the legality of the research content. The application then distributes the finished research piece to eight different content aggregators—Bloomberg and Thompson Financial's FirstCall, for example.

O'Connor notes that Putnam Lovell wanted to use Web services to start distributing research directly to its clients—individual institutional investors—rather than supplying its information through external content aggregators.

> We have a CRM system—Salesforce.com—that's also Internet-based. We use Salesforce.com to keep track of all our contacts and companies. Within the application, each employee tracks whether or not the client wants to receive research, and what type of research he wants to receive.
>
> BlueMatrix has the content, and Salesforce.com has the client's interest profile. The challenge that we had was to connect to the two independently managed and distributed systems to enable the content to be automatically sent to those clients that had a specific interest.

To link BlueMatrix with Salesforce.com, Putnam Lovell uses a network-based service provided by Grand Central Communications.

> Grand Central is also an Internet-based application, which we subscribe to as a service. We do not have any server or software running on our network, but we configure their service to have a connector between BlueMatrix and Salesforce.com. Within the Grand Central network, we can configure the security rules to specify the type of data that is allowed to pass between the two applications.

Early on, Putnam Lovell relied on "screen scraping"—acquiring data displayed on screen by capturing the characters with a utility. Screen scraping has long been used to save meaningful data for later use. However, distributing data elements into identifiable fields for database processing must be done manually, or via intelligence built into a specialized software utility. As more text on Web pages is defined by XML tags, the job of transferring data elements into databases and between applications can be made more automatic.

> We initially used Grand Central to screen scrape Salesforce.com. Then, about two months after we went into production, Salesforce.com released their direct XML API. We could then build another connector in Grand Central to point to Salesforce.com's XML API.

Although Salesforce.com now supports XML, Grand Central is still highly useful as an intermediary.

> We could have built a point-to-point connection, but there are several advantages to having a proxy service. For one, it isolates each vendor's connection from changes at the other. We have seen several examples of this. For example, Salesforce.com changed its protocol and implemented its API in a new way. We developed an additional connector from Grand Central to Salesforce.com's new API. We tested it to make sure it was correct, and then switched over from the old way to the new way without any intervention from BlueMatrix.
>
> Proxying the interface made the whole process more resilient and cheaper to maintain. It reduced the cost of ownership, as you do not have to get everybody

> involved. Grand Central also provides reporting, e-mail notification of errors, and security.

Taking advantage of new features, as software vendors offer them, is key to deriving the maximum value out of Web services, says O'Connor.

> Salesforce.com is coming out with a SOAP–based interface within the next few months. On average, I would expect each vendor to change some aspect of its API each year.

O'Connor notes that the real power of an integration hub, like Grand Central, becomes apparent as more applications are added to the Web services implementation.

> The real benefit is when you add multiple applications, for example, when a third application needs to be integrated with either of the existing nodes. You would just have to add a connector to the new application. The connection and security of the other two application connections can be reused.

An integration hub can also simplify a complex Web services arrangement, says O'Connor.

> Say you have six applications, with each application talking to three others—you end up with a rat's nest of connections, where it could become very expensive to replace or upgrade any application. If you proxy the connection to a single location, it makes the process of change much simpler.

For Putnam Lovell, the introduction of Web services marked a major change from the way the firm used to handle information distribution. As a result of its Web services initiative, Putnam Lovell has been able to slice its $40,000 quarterly budget for information distribution in half.

> We produce a lot of printed research. Part of the Web services effort was to move from printed to electronic content and distribution of research. One of the drivers was reducing the cost of printing and mailing. It doesn't cost you anything if you find there's been a change of address, for example.

Converting its information distribution process over to Web services was a carefully planned process, says O'Connor.

> The first step was to use the Internet to provision our generic enterprise applications in early 2000. That excluded actual transaction applications, such as our trading platforms and our communications, which we kept inside the firewall. With every generic application, we looked to provision via an Internet-based service, rather than the traditional strategy of owning and looking after the software. Down that path, we implemented BlueMatrix, Salesforce.com, and several other components of our application infrastructures. We wanted to outsource our nonfinancial transaction applications wherever it made sense.
>
> Because we followed this strategy, we could not follow the normal path of integration by utilizing direct

> database-to-database connections. We didn't have visibility to the database layer, only to vendor-provided APIs into the application.

Implementing the system was fast and relatively painfree, says O'Connor.

> We went live in September 2001. It took four weeks to get the first business process automated. It went very quickly.

Web services also helps Putnam Lovell clients find information on their own.

> BlueMatrix provides a client research library on our Web site. Clients can log in with a user name and password and see all of the research that we've published. They can access recent reports, or search for all content on a particular company.
>
> We control permission to access the library via a custom field in Salesforce.com. An employee can very easily set up a client to have access. The integration is using the same Grand Central network as the research distribution process. It was very simple for us to reuse the configuration from the first process to enable the second—approximately eight hours of development.

O'Connor says he doesn't worry too much about Web standards, since they're beyond his control. He has resisted the temptation to try any features that are on the extreme cutting edge.

> I am using very low-level Web services standards—such as SOAP and XML. I'm using my own dialect of XML because the dataset is very simple, and I control both the producer and consumer of the content. I'm not using ebXML or riXML to define research.
>
> Since we are using XML as a standard, we can use XML tools to examine and manipulate the data. We are using SOAP where we can. The standards I'm using are lower down the stack, and hence, well defined and unlikely to change. The confusion seems to be higher up the stack in the areas of security and transaction control.

Error handling and asynchronous messaging can be pitfalls for novice Web services developers, says O'Connor.

> Traditionally, this kind of integration would be via a synchronous RPC. So you've got to make sure your developers understand that they have to handle errors and asynchronous messaging somewhat differently.
>
> For example, application A starts query one, "I want to know X," and then disconnects. It then sends query two, "I want to know Y." It may not get the return sets back in the same order that it requested them. The first answer it may get back is, "This is Y." Or, it may get something back saying, "I can't give you Y—there's an error giving you Y." So you've got to make sure that your calls—what it's asking for and what it gets back—are correlated. You have to make sure that the error handling is set up to cope with the time differences between your queries and replies.

Security, says O'Connor, is also an important consideration, particularly when dealing with critical proprietary research information. Fortunately, the implementation he designed has built-in safeguards.

> We're relying on Grand Central to reduce the complexity of security. BlueMatrix doesn't have visibility into the Salesforce.com. BlueMatrix authenticates to Grand Central, and uses SSL to encrypt authentication and session data.
>
> We configure Grand Central to allow BlueMatrix to initiate specific queries into the Salesforce.com connector. It then authenticates to Salesforce.com, and again communicates over an SSL–encrypted session.
>
> It's interesting, because none of these applications are on my side of the firewall. Everything is on the Internet. Each one is an island with its own secure perimeter. BlueMatrix can't talk to Salesforce.com directly, it can only talk to Grand Central, and Grand Central has tight security between it and both vendors: BlueMatrix and Salesforce.com.

O'Connor admits, however, that this arrangement probably wouldn't be secure enough for an enterprise engaged in financial transactions.

> As a conscious decision, I would not put financial transactions over the same mechanism.

A strong advocate of Web services, O'Connor believes that the technology is ready for widespread use.

> I would recommend it for application-to-application integration, where you control all the points of integration. It's a much more controllable environment than a one-to-many integration, or opening up internal legacy systems to anybody coming in from the Internet. That's a very different scenario than integrating two applications that are already built natively for the Internet.

He feels that Web services are also suitable for exchanging data with business partners, although he advocates starting small.

> It depends on how many vendors you have, and the amount of resource you are willing to dedicate. I would recommend starting with a manageable number of parties, and, once operational, expand the quantity of connection points. Historically, if you had a requirement to electronically transmit content to your suppliers, your options were limited to expensive EDI or quick and dirty FTP that's relatively easy to set up, but very expensive to manage going forward. Today you have an alternative of using Web services, and using a service like Grand Central to manage the connections for you.

Down the road, O'Connor sees emerging Web services technologies providing a path to new types of applications.

> Some of the emerging standards are very interesting. I think the WS process and the WS security are going to open a lot of applications and new uses.

O'Connor feels that the Web services market will eventually be dominated by major software players.

> I think the larger ones are tying it up pretty well. IBM certainly seems to be investing a lot into this. And then, there's Microsoft with its .NET initiative. Sun seems to be trying to catch up.
>
> I've been watching the field very closely for the last couple of years. It started off with some of the smaller, emerging companies who were doing some very interesting things—and I think they will continue to have a position in certain niches. But the larger players are setting the direction of the standards.

O'Connor advises IT managers to start small and to pick their Web services projects carefully.

> I would suggest trying to pick small integration projects to act as good learning exercises.

The global recession has set back many Web services projects, says O'Connor.

> There have been a lot of pilot projects. I think lots of those were probably hit by the recession, so maybe they didn't get from pilot to widespread adoption because of the economy.

As Web services become more popular, it will become easier for enterprises to implement the technology, says O'Connor.

> It will become more and more of a standard. We are starting to see off-the-shelf applications and services that include Web services APIs. I think you'll probably see a large number of them blossom over the next twenty-four months. I think one of the catalysts to this adoption will be new XML–based offerings from Microsoft, such as Office 2003 and xDocs.

Microsoft InfoPath (formerly code-named XDocs) is a new product in the Microsoft Office family that streamlines the process of gathering information by enabling teams and organizations to easily create and work with rich, dynamic forms. The information collected can be integrated with a broad range of business processes because InfoPath supports any customer-defined XML schema and integrates with XML Web services. As a result, InfoPath helps to connect information workers directly to organizational information. It gives them the ability to act on it, which leads to greater business impact.

Chapter 3

Hewlett-Packard—Web Services on Multiple Fronts

Hewlett-Packard (HP) is a leading global provider of products, technologies, solutions, and services to consumers and business. The company's offerings span IT infrastructure, personal computing and access devices, global services, and imaging and printing. HP's $4 billion annual research and development investment fuels the invention of products, solutions, and new technologies. The May 2002 merger of Hewlett-Packard and Compaq Computer Corporation forged a dynamic, powerful team of 140,000 employees with capabilities in 160 countries, doing business in forty-three currencies and fifteen languages. Revenues for the combined companies were $72 billion for the fiscal year that ended October 31, 2002. Chairman and CEO Carly Fiorina leads HP, which has corporate headquarters in Palo Alto, California.

HP consists of four core business groups:

1. *The Enterprise Systems Group (ESG).* ESG focuses on providing the key technology components of en-

terprise IT infrastructure to enhance business agility, including enterprise storage, servers, management software, and a variety of solutions.

2. *The Imaging and Printing Group (IPG).* HP is the leading provider of printing and imaging solutions for both business and consumers. IPG includes printer hardware, all-in-ones, digital imaging devices, such as cameras and scanners, and associated supplies and accessories. It also is expanding into the commercial printing market.
3. *HP Services (HPS).* HP Services is a premier, global IT services team. It offers guidance, know-how, and a comprehensive portfolio of services to help customers realize measurable business value from their IT investment.
4. *The Personal Systems Group (PSG).* PSG focuses on providing simple, reliable, and affordable personal-computing solutions and devices for home and business use, including desktop and notebook PCs, workstations, thin clients, smart handhelds, and personal devices.

In addition to the four business groups, HP Labs provides a central research function for the company. HP Labs is focused on inventing new technologies that change markets and create business opportunities.

Recently merged with Compaq Computer, Hewlett-Packard stands as a global information systems titan. The company is number one in servers, external storage, and printing and imaging in terms of market share. In the services business, HP has moved from around number seven to one of the industry powerhouses, sitting at the number three position. The company's personal systems unit continues to sell both HP and Compaq products to consumers and all types of businesses. HP's formidable enterprise systems group includes servers, storage systems, and software. The company vies with IBM, Dell, and Sun Microsystems at the top of the server market, with products based on the Microsoft platform, as well as UNIX- and Linux-based offerings. While HP is best known for its computer technologies, printing and imaging is very important to the company, and it is its most profitable sector.

Mike Baker is HP's information technology officer. Baker joined Compaq in 1990. His initial assignments were in the Compaq Systems Engineering Group, and he has held management positions in the company's IT unit since 1992. Prior to joining Compaq, Baker worked for Baxter Heathcare and American Hospital Supply (AHS). His experience at Baxter and AHS spanned a number of IT management roles, including assignments in system architecture, telecommunications, database administration, and application development. He participated in the development of AHS's ASAP system, a predecessor to today's e-commerce technology.

A strong Web services advocate, Baker believes that the technology and its associated open standards mark the next wave in computing. Baker notes that HP has been deeply involved in Web services almost since the technology's inception.

> We have been exploring Web services since early 2000 and have been participating actively in the standards bodies, including W3C, UDDI, WS-I, and so on.

Currently, we have a variety of internally and externally exposed Web services in production, including:

- Product configuration and price checks
- Product catalog information
- Payment authorization and fraud checking
- Tax calculation
- Product contract and warranty information
- Field services dispatching
- Enterprise application integration
- B2B integration

One of the attractions of Web services to us is that this is really a standards-based addition that allows a new level of interoperability between applications, both within the corporation and outside the four walls of the corporation. With Web services, because they are based on standards, any individual vendor's product isn't critically important to us. Yes, we make decisions about which particular products to do specific implementations on, but the interoperability we're able to achieve is the key foundation stone.

Most companies recognize that a single ERP solution doesn't provide all the functionality that's needed. The ideal is to implement best-of-breed, composite applications that snap on to an existing heterogeneous IT environment and create seamless, cross-functional business processes. The same is true with Web services. We have currently implemented functionality, as Web services are needed, in

> many places and by many applications. Even though the data provided is not necessarily new, the way it is encapsulated and provided as central services is. We are also thinking about brand-new business models that could be supported using Web services.

For HP, Web services have provided a new, more effective way to build bridges between applications.

> Before Web services were defined, we solved application integration challenges by using vendor-provided application adapters, like BEA eLink services and SAP's Business Connector. We also implemented a ZLE solution (HP's Zero Latency Enterprise real-time integration framework) on Himalaya, which serves as a message hub for important supply chain documents, using the publish once/subscribe many paradigm. Now, the Himalaya integration can be easily exposed as Web services.

Baker appreciates the technically agnostic orientation of Web services.

> Web services enable us to implement business functionality in a technically agnostic way. This allows us to select the most efficient technology solutions that leverage our existing investments and provide the easiest integration. We're able, for example, to quickly wrap our BEA eLink integration calls with SOAP interfaces and call them from any hardware and OS platform—without having to spend anything on proprietary messaging middleware. The technical agnosticism that Web services provide reduces the

cost of technology investments to reach the business-to-business market, and it enables communication with divergent technologies. It's easy to use and implement.

The modular nature of Web services enables us to leverage the benefits of distributed computing without the technical complications inherent in the currently used distributed object models. The use of Web services for such ubiquitous internal processes as tax calculations, currency conversions, or freight calculations allows for a single source of code maintenance and upgrade when business rules, or needs, change. Any and all applications that require these pieces of business functionality will be able to simply consume the available internally or externally hosted Web services.

The Web services paradigm has the potential to deliver many benefits for internal application integration, as well as interaction with external customers and partners. The Web services framework holds promise in several areas of software development and application integration. In theory, the Web services framework can enable new methods for creating and delivering application functionality, including:

- *Modular Applications*. Developers can divide applications into smaller components for delivery as Web services software. Higher-level applications can aggregate and orchestrate the flow of data and logic between multiple Web services software components.
- *Reuse*. Developers can expose internal application functions for reuse by other network end points. A de-

veloper can reuse a single Web service software component, such as a sales tax calculator, in multiple application flows. Hewlett-Packard might also be able to purchase or subscribe to Web services, which would fit our buy-versus-build principle.

- *Choice*. Multiple Web services software components can provide identical application functionality, such as tax calculation. Choosing a different supplier for a particular function should not affect other Web services software components, as long as the interfaces those components use remain the same.
- *Self-Describing*. At the core of Web services is XML. Documents in XML describe the interfaces, formats, and functions of software components, which humans, applications, or other software components can parse and understand.
- *Interoperability Without Dependencies*. Because the Web services framework uses XML–based specifications, it doesn't mandate the underlying hardware platform, operating system, development environment, or application server. Thus, the framework is ideal for application and data integration between dissimilar systems. The Web services framework brings these benefits to applications, even monolithic applications that support the framework.
- *New Value-Delivery Channels*. There are many opportunities for HP to provide new services delivered over the Web, which will enhance user experience and satisfaction. The framework also provides a directory for advertising and discovering applications published as Web services software.

- *New Business Models*. The Web services framework has the potential to break down the barriers to interenterprise application interoperability. As such, the framework has the potential to provide the technological foundation for a new way of integrating partners, suppliers, and, ultimately, customers into the business process.

> The Web service paradigm is about interoperability and platform-neutral communications, as opposed to a specific development language, component model, and platform issues. This is in contrast to CORBA, COM, and EJB, which allow platform interoperability, but have proprietary component models and binary wire formats for distributed information communication.

Given its deep involvement in Web services, HP is utilizing a diverse array of technologies.

> As expected in a newly merged company, we're using several technologies. We have the intention to streamline this portfolio. Since we expect to implement J2EE–based applications as well as .NET solutions, interoperability (provided by using industry standards) is very important to us. These standards include:
>
> - Microsoft Visual Studio .NET and Framework
> - Borland JBuilder for J2EE applications
> - BEA WebLogic (selected as the J2EE application server technology)

- Borland Control Center (a development platform)
- Eclipse 1.0 (an open-source, integrated development environment)
- Jboss (an open-source application server)

HP is taking a centralized approach to Web services development.

> We've created a cross-departmental virtual Web Services Center. It defines strategy, recommendations, and road maps for all aspects of the Web services architecture for Hewlett-Packard IT. In this collaborative, coordinated effort we are looking at specific business opportunities, shared business Web services, central infrastructure components, security, policies and standards, and Web services hosting and management aspects.
>
> Adopting Web services doesn't require completely changing your current infrastructure. We're using an evolutionary approach, wrapping legacy applications with SOAP, starting with sending simple XML messaging over HTTP, gradually moving to a stricter definition of a Web service that adheres to all industry standards. It's important to move to a service-oriented architecture first, since components can be easily turned into pure Web services at a later point in time. Implementing a services-oriented architecture requires an attitude change, though. Components need to be designed and developed in a way that allows for sharing.

Baker feels that HP's early Web services investments are already providing a return.

> The early adoption of Web services has already paid back—we've developed knowledge and experience. It's now a matter of explaining the value and possible return on investment (ROI) to businesspeople. The definition of Web services has been changing, and it is still not used in the same sense by everybody. In the beginning, we used a very loose definition—every software component that could be called using XML over HTTP was considered a Web service. Now that some basic standards like SOAP and WSDL are out, we can easily turn them into Web services that meet a tighter, industry standard–based definition.

One way HP utilizes Web services is through Comprehensive Web Solutions (CWS), a Web application that allows suppliers that aren't EDI–enabled to receive EDI communications transmitted by HP.

> The Web application allows vendors to receive and acknowledge supplier-related EDI signals after logging into HP's secure supplier extranet. The EDI signals are transmitted between SAP and CWS, via XML documents through EIA Services. The XML document structures represent the standard SAP IDOC format.
>
> The CWS model presented in Figure 1 shows the process relationships between HP's ERP (SAP) systems and its supplier base. The simplified process narrative is as follows:

Figure 1. Process flow of HP's Comprehensive Web Solutions (CWS) model.

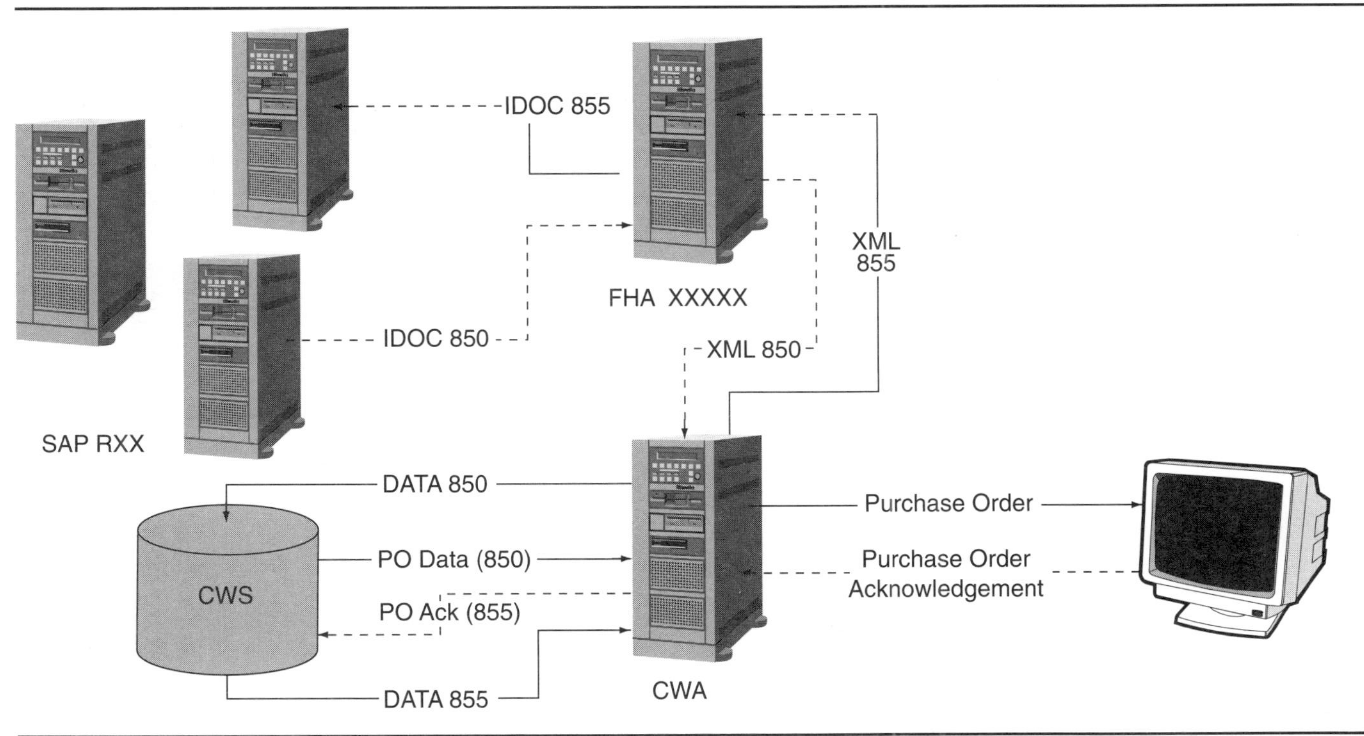

- Hewlett-Packard generates an SAP purchase order for goods or services from one of its suppliers. The exchange is first initiated as SAP standard Intermediate Document (IDOC). This is translated into an 850 XML document, based on the structure of the outbound IDOC. (This process is also repeated in the same manner for 824 signals, which are acknowledgment signals for 856 and 810 signals received from the vendor.)
- SAP forwards the XML 850 to EIA Services.
- EIA Services sends the XML document to CWS via an HTTP post transaction.
- Comprehensive Web Solutions validates the content of the 850 XML document.
- The validated 850 XML data is passed to the CWS SQL Server 2000 database, where a stored procedure parses and maps the XML document to an in-memory tree structure that represents the nodes in the document. The document's contents are then shredded to facilitate mapping the node's elements to specific tables within the CWS database for record insertion or modification.
- The supplier logs into HP's secure supplier extranet to access the CWS application and is presented with a display of all purchase orders assigned to the company's SAP supplier code.
- The supplier reviews and acknowledges the purchase orders.

- The purchase order acknowledgment data is immediately generated by constructing an XML template to retrieve the data directly into XML document fragments. The data retrieved by the template also applies the signal-specific XSLT style sheet to produce the 855 XML document structure for the SAP IDOC message. (This procedure is also repeated for these additional signals: 856, Goods Issue, and 810.)
- Comprehensive Web Solutions forwards the 855 XML document to the EIA Service via an HTTP post transaction.
- EIA Services sends the 855 XML to the appropriate SAP environment.
- SAP retrieves, validates, and finally posts the acknowledgement.

Baker says CWS marks a big improvement over the technology it replaced.

> Previously, these processes were handled by an application distributed to the targeted vendors. Called Harbinger, it was developed by Peregrine Systems. The application was installed on the supplier's system, and it followed traditional EDI processes to send and receive EDI signals in the standard X12 industry standard format. The VAN was still used to broker the EDI signals between HP and the vendor. In some cases, a paperwork solution was still implemented between HP and the vendor.

Comprehensive Web Solutions offers benefits on multiple levels, notes Baker.

> Web Services provides several benefits over traditional EDI services. The greatest is bypassing the VAN. The VAN is a third-party interface that brokers the EDI signals between partners. Traditional EDI required HP to FTP the EDI document to the VAN, which routed it to the appropriate vendor's queue. The vendor retrieved the signal when it logged into the VAN. The service provided by the VAN was very costly, and it isn't needed using Web services.
>
> The primary benefits of CWS are:
>
> - Efficiency of development and maintenance, especially when multiple applications must be interconnected
> - Design to industry standards (such as RosettaNet), where applicable, to permit exposure and brokering of the services
> - Isolation of the vendor-specific platform, so that the implementation can be changed without affecting other applications
> - Less complicated support, since all the hardware belongs to HP
> - Reuse and knowledge leveraging across multiple architectures, development teams, and projects
> - Fast and inexpensive integration of new suppliers, without the need to invest in additional software on the supplier's side

Security is fundamental to CWS, says Baker.

> All communications require SSL. User authorization to the Web front end is handled through the supplier extranet. Comprehensive Web Solutions also handles user privacy by filtering data content according to HP's privacy regulations.

Baker believes that security is critical to a successful Web services implementation.

> Not surprisingly, there's more sensitivity to security today than there ever has been in the past. I've been in the industry for twenty-five years, and security was almost nonexistent very early in my career. Concepts about security, while they were developed to some degree, were rarely implemented.
>
> The situation is certainly changed today for a lot of reasons. Now, we're very sensitized to the importance of security. When we talk about Web services, we consider it to be a pivot point in the way that we deliver IT services, and we just want to pay a tremendous amount of attention to security from the start. We hope to avoid, quite frankly, some of the problems we've had in the past, where we needed to retrofit security into existing systems.
>
> I don't think all of this is any great surprise to anyone who follows the industry. If you look at what's going on in the Web-based application frameworks, there's a fair amount of pretty obvious scrambling going on to fix up issues in security. Certainly, there's been a lot of commentary about Microsoft's problems in

> security—it's almost become comical about the number of different security patches they're releasing for their product line. It's also true in the open source world that there's a pretty continuous churn of trying to close down exposures.
>
> So, if we look at using these technologies now, we're really kind of coming up the stack a layer or two, and we're looking at it from an application perspective for the applications we're providing. But, in our program efforts with Web services, we're saying that security needs to be designed from the start. We don't want to go through another one of these generations of retrofit.

Baker is highly pleased with the way the rollout has proceeded.

> Our Web services experience has been very satisfactory. New development environments are making creation and implementation really easy. But, to achieve the full benefits of Web services, we need to change to a service-oriented architecture as well, which offers several challenges—organizational and design-related changes, as well as technical and operational ones. It's a paradigm shift: Instead of thinking and implementing in "silos," we're moving to a culture of sharing and reuse. That starts with providing an environment and tools for people to find out what's being developed or implemented in the company. An internal UDDI registry, as well as an XML schema repository, design guidelines, and processes for rolling out truly shared Web services, is

> really needed. An internal UDDI repository is currently in pilot mode and will be in production soon.

Web services are definitely an improvement over traditional middleware solutions, notes Baker.

> Web services make cross-platform integrations a lot easier: Instead of buying proprietary middleware, we were able to use Web services to integrate different OS platforms, thus saving license and maintenance costs. Our configuration Web services provide a single, definitive rules engine utilizing SAP IPC, which can be used by a variety of applications that need product configuration information. This ensures delivering consistent results, regardless of the application that makes the call and saves. Another benefit is the integration of smaller, external business partners who wouldn't have been able to invest in a comprehensive EDI infrastructure. Web services allow them to submit their business documents, including invoices, shipments, and confirmations, using industry standard components and the Internet, without having to make huge infrastructure investments.

Baker believes the business potential of Web services hasn't yet been fully exploited. Nevertheless, he's looking forward to taking advantage of future Web services technologies.

> We certainly don't see many "killer apps" on the market that clearly demonstrate the business opportunities the Web services paradigm provides. Microsoft's myServices vision, which allows for subscription-

> based functionality, hasn't really taken off yet. We're seeing vendors exposing the functionality of their application packages as Web services, and we applaud this, since it will make application integration a lot easier. It also will be helpful to review more successful business cases and to develop better ways of determining the ROI of Web services–based solutions. The availability of key, enabling Web services, such as microbilling, subscription management, and security functions, will further help the rollout of a services-oriented architecture.

Baker believes that, despite existing limitations, Web services are definitely ready for everyday use.

> We would like to see better processes and tools to help the management of Web services, from the business level to the infrastructure, especially the security aspect. But this doesn't preclude us from further rolling out a services-oriented architecture and using Web services in internal enterprise application integration and, in selected cases, offering exposure to the external world.

Baker feels that a Web services initiative requires a full organizational commitment. He suggests that businesses create an internal Web services task force.

> Establish a Web services center of expertise, which can start as a virtual team. Then, develop an enterprise-wide vision and road map of the implementation. Start with exploring the business opportunities of Web services, and communicate them. Build a re-

> pository of business Web service examples. Develop road maps and guidelines for all architectural layers—ROI calculation algorithms, design and development guidelines, central infrastructure services, and security aspects—built around the hosting strategy. Determine your priorities for a rollout of Web services, and focus on a couple of pilots. Facilitate knowledge and experience sharing through internal Web services community events and training sessions.

Web services aren't particularly easy to implement, notes Baker, but they also don't present any insurmountable obstacles.

> It's going to take some diligence and some follow-through. Anytime you introduce new technologies in IT, you're going to have failures and successes in the appropriate use of the new technology. We need to be rational about that, and we need to exercise diligence processes to really assess each one of these early exercises. We need to assess how successful these processes actually are at delivering against the total vision. Then, you may want to take some corrective action to bring them in line. But it's not going to be easy, and there's a lot to change management that needs to go on.

Baker offers some final thoughts.

> We consider Web services to be the next wave in computing. It's really early in its life cycle, particularly in terms of deployment activity, but there's a lot

of power in standards-based approaches. It's a lot more powerful than some things that we've seen in the past. We, as a corporation, are embracing Web services. They're going to make a very durable and long run.

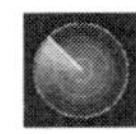

Chapter 4

Vail Resorts—Traveling with Web Services

Based in Avon, Colorado, Vail Resorts is one of North America's leading resort operators.

Vail's operations are grouped into three segments—mountain, lodging, and real estate—which represent 65 percent, 25 percent, and 10 percent, respectively, of the company's revenues for the 2002 fiscal year. The company owns and operates four ski resorts in Colorado, a ski resort in Lake Tahoe, California, and a summer resort in Grand Teton, Wyoming. Additionally, the company recently acquired a majority interest in Rock Resorts, which manages ten luxury resort hotels across the United States.

Vail's resorts and resort hotels are designed to provide a comprehensive vacation experience throughout the year to a diverse clientele that features a high-end demographic profile. Vail, Beaver Creek, Breckenridge, and Keystone, all located within Colorado, are year-round mountain resorts offering a full range of on-snow and off-snow activities. Heavenly, which is located on the south shore of Lake Tahoe, was acquired in May 2002, making it the fifth resort in the company's portfolio of premier U.S. ski resorts. Over the next five years, Vail Resorts plans to invest $40 million at Heavenly in on-mountain resort improvements including upgrading the existing facilities, building new restaurants, and upgrading or replacing lifts and snowmaking systems, as well as enhancing the resort's environmental efforts.

Vail's resorts and resort hotels derive revenue through a comprehensive offering of amenities, including resort accommodations, lift ticket sales, ski and snowboard lesson packages, retail and equipment rental outlets, dining venues, mountain biking, golf, and private club operations. Other recreational activities include tennis, horseback riding, fishing tours, float trips, and on-mountain activities centers. Besides providing extensive guest conveniences, the company also engages in commercial leasing of restaurant, retail, and other commercial space, real estate brokerage services, and extensive licensing and sponsorship activities with brand-name companies. The firm's wholly owned subsidiary, Vail Resorts Development Co., develops, buys, and sells real estate in and around resort communities.

Vail is using Web services technologies to manage travel reservations over the Internet. The company's leisure travel booking system enables its resorts and resort hotels, as well as destination management organizations and travel and transportation suppliers, to assemble a broad range of travel inventories and destination content for Internet distribution. The booking system is also designed to provide dynamic packaging and connectivity to inventory management systems.

Vail, in partnership with software developer Datalex, created its Web services–driven booking system in order to boost online travel sales and to improve the efficiency of its sales operations (see Figure 2). The design objectives aimed to:

- Encompass all travel components available in one system.
- Enable online packages to be created dynamically.
- Implement promotions rapidly through dynamic pricing and rules capabilities.
- Enable a seamless booking transaction process from purchaser through supplier.
- Increase sales productivity, sales retention, and booking efficiency, while lowering operating costs.

The system's initial phase is available on Vail's Web site (www.snow.com). The service offers visitors robust search, selection, and purchasing functionalities across the represented inventories. The technologies allow travel suppliers to aggregate and package multiple product types, including traditional air, car, and hotel products, with leisure activities such as spa visits, golfing, and skiing.

The system uses an extensible Web Services framework that's enriched with XML messaging. The system allows components to be sold from an array of air, lodging, car rental, ground transportation, activi-

Figure 2. Datalex's leisure travel booking solution conducts component sales from an array of air, lodging, car rental, ground transportation, activities, shows, and attractions.

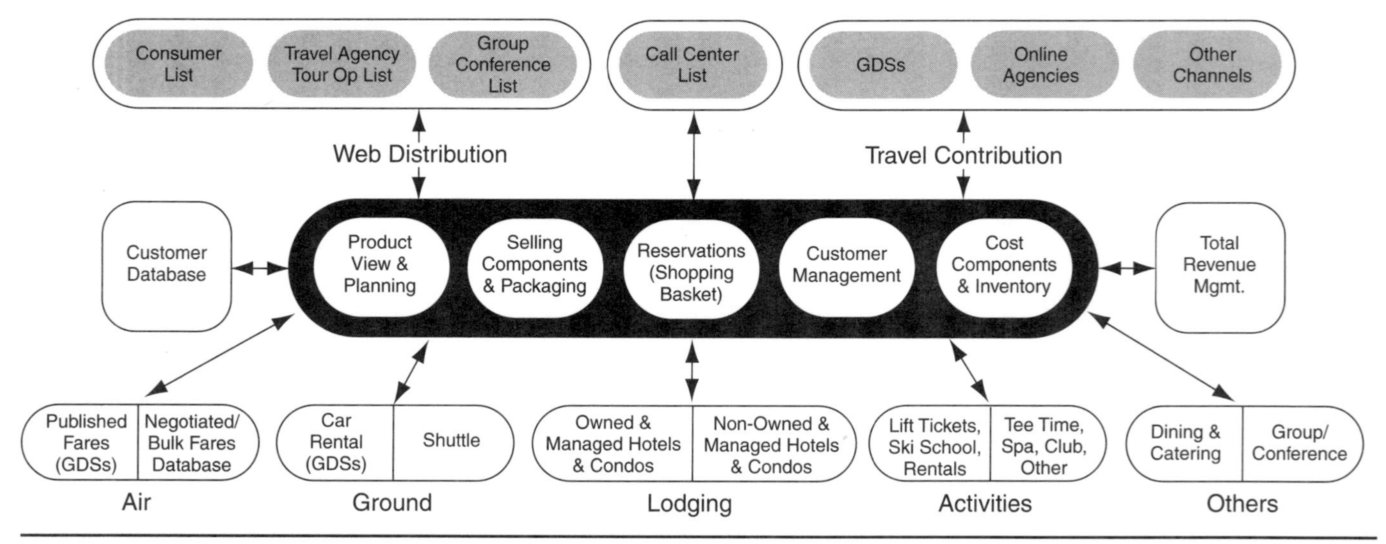

ties, shows, and attraction suppliers, each in adherence with complex package-selling rules and restrictions. It also provides support for promotional rates and packaging. Product and reservations requests are directed to the appropriate host inventory source, according to rules established in the system's database. This feature permits connectivity to existing central reservations, or property management systems, for real-time lodging rates and inventory information, and to aggregate this information with rich content, managed and served from the system's database. The product supports connectivity, via legacy system adapters, to the major global distribution systems for selling air transportation and car rentals.

The travel distribution system's functional highlights include:

- *Content.* This includes detail-rich product information, including extended multilanguage descriptions of the product, as well as destination information.
- *Searches.* This includes regional, price-based, amenity, attribute, and unit type, with ranked results.
- *Packaging.* This provides dynamic, à la carte, and prebuilt components that are available online.
- *Dynamic Rules Engine.* This allows administrators to create new rules for promotions, pricing, inventory, and packaging and to rapidly implement targeted and seasonal discounts.
- *Connectivity.* This makes the system capable of making dynamic calls to locally held inventory on suppliers' own PMS/CRS systems and to selected external systems for availability and pricing.

- *Air Fares.* This provides access to private-fare pricing and availability, using Datalex's BookIt! Fares software.

Martin White is Vail's senior vice president for marketing and sales. White joined the company in October 2000. Previously, beginning in 1998, White served as vice president of consumer marketing for Delta Air Lines at its Atlanta headquarters. From July 1997 to November 1998, White was vice president of marketing programs and services with US Airways. White began his career in 1987 at Continental Airlines, where he held several management positions. In 1991 he joined Brierley & Partners, a Dallas-based marketing firm, where he headed the company's work with United Airlines and was later named senior vice president of the international division, based in Chicago.

White says the Vail's Web services partnership with Datalex draws on each company's strengths.

> We built the whole engine in conjunction with Datalex. We built the front end and the user interface while they provided all the middleware. Some of the system pulls directly from Datalex's other products—they're the back end behind Orbitz, for example.

White notes that the booking system was designed to appeal to the well-heeled and technologically savvy type of person the company typically attracts.

> Over 90 percent of our guests have access to the Internet, which isn't surprising, given the fact that we deal with very affluent guests. Of those people with

> access, we've surveyed that 80 percent were actually doing some form of research on the Internet prior to booking their ski vacation. That's also not surprising, given the complications associated with a ski vacation. It's much harder to plan and book a ski vacation than it would be, for instance, to go and lie on the beach in Florida somewhere. You've got a lot of different package components, you've got to understand proximities to lifts and village layouts, and things like that. It's much different than a lot of beach resorts. Many of the nice beach resorts, which are very simple to book, are in close proximity to a major metro area.

White notes that implementing Snow.com generated an immediate and very positive impact on sales.

> Previously, we did about 11 percent or 12 percent of our bookings online. To date this year [Spring 2003], with the advent of the new online booking engine, we've already doubled that number. We've taken 11 percent to 22 percent.

Snow.com is very consumer-oriented, says White.

> Although lots of travel agents and various providers around the travel industry use Snow.com, it's primarily focused as a consumer site. If you're booking on Snow.com, we act as a tour wholesaler. We're also a consolidator in that we communicate and sell a lot of third-party products on that site. For example, Vail Cascade, which is a large lodging property in Vail, gives us rooms inventory. We basically have a stan-

> dard relationship with them where the customer pays us, and we sell Cascade's rooms. The Cascade actually ends up paying us a commission.

Web services allow Vail to automate its various Web site transactions, including room, air, and rental car reservations.

> The best example is the Hertz part of the reservation. We would automatically confirm your Hertz reservations for you. We end up booking the car with Hertz. We get a confirmation number, and then that's conveyed through us as part of your overall vacation confirmation.

White says the technology provides benefits to both Vail and its customers.

> Primarily, for the consumer, it means more inventory, more choices. For us, inventory management and yield management are the two big gains we've made in launching this product. We can manage down to the last room availability. We can change prices on a daily basis. We're running it so we don't have to work with a third-party provider to provide them access or provide them inventory, and then we have to wait for them to load it. We just do it ourselves—it's all hooked into our back end.
>
> There's also going to be a lot of CRM capabilities on this booking engine, some of which have already been loaded. We've got a database here at Vail Resorts: If you're in that, then it can pull a lot of information straight from the database.

The introduction of Web services was a big change, as well as a major challenge, for Vail.

> We've basically taken the biggest initiative in the industry to go off and actually develop this proprietary software. Just four years ago, most people were still booking via the telephone.

Susan Rubin-Stewart, Vail's director of reservations, says a custom-designed front end makes site navigation very easy.

> We call it VCUI—the Vail Consumer User Interface. The front end is written in ASP and communicates in XML to the Datalex portion.
>
> We call the entire system RIBE—the Reservation Internet Booking Engine. It's comprised of "servants" and a database. That's what the Datalex product is. There's the database and then there's the processing part, which is what they call servants. The servants use the database and make the calls, deliver information to the front end, and receive information for the back end.

Today's system is the result of a two-year development process, says Rubin-Stewart.

> I'd say it's two years of my life. A lot of it also has to do with the functionality and requirements for a full-blown reservations system. So about a year of my time was spent solely on development.

The system, says Rubin-Stewart, began as a consolidation project, and then evolved into something much more sophisticated.

> Initially, we were looking to replace a lot of disparate systems. We had more than one reservation system, and we were trying to centralize data entry, distribution, and so forth. So, actually, it was a big project to begin with. It replaced all of our reservation technology and Web-enabled it.

Datalex was brought into the picture after Vail realized it couldn't handle the job on its own, notes Rubin-Stewart.

> It became a joint venture, because there wasn't any software that supported our vision. We partnered with Datalex and actually created a joint venture to produce and sell the software.
>
> The Internet portion is very complicated. Replacing your entire reservation system adds additional complex programming to support hosted inventory, accounting, etc.

Vail worked closely with Resort Technology Partners (RTP), a joint venture with Vail Resorts. RTP, located in Avon, Colorado, specializes in software and Internet services for the resort industry. Rubin-Stewart says close cooperation was critical to designing an environment that would serve the needs of both Vail and its customers.

> We worked with RTP. They had an information architect and usability designer. On the front end, we de-

> veloped a page schematic, which represented the kind of flow we would like. We had done surveys of customers who had booked online last year through WorldRes (a Web-based hotel reservations system that includes properties operated by Vail and other companies) among people who bailed out and called us on the phone. What we found was that our customers were pretty evenly divided between those who wanted to assemble a packaged vacation by themselves and those who wanted something very simple—just press a button, and we make recommendations for them.
>
> We sat down with the information architect/designer and really talked about the differences and how we could support both flows. It was definitely like a group working together. We worked closely.

System implementation generated few problems, says White.

> It was the normal new product integration and rollout type of scenario. There were some bumps and surprises. As the product was developed, we tried to overcome most of the problems as they arose. But you can't catch everything through testing. Some minor launch problems occurred—mostly with functionality on the sites and on the booking engine. They've been very minor to this point.

Rubin-Stewart says the system implementation difficulties were normal and of the type to be expected for any large development and integration project.

> Anyone thinking of getting into this type of project should be aware of the complexities of the project, and expect a lot of hard work, coordination, problem solving, and compromises.

Rubin-Stewart compares the project to the task of burrowing a tunnel between Britain and France.

> It was kind of like digging the Chunnel. Actually, that was the expression we used—"The Chunnel." There were times we missed things by about a foot—just like the Chunnel itself was slightly off on its trajectory. This is pretty minor, however, when you consider the scope of the project—theirs and ours. In any case, whenever a problem arose, the engine or the front end had to be modified to make it work.
>
> One area we were all pretty new at was determining the likely user volume and architecting the hardware to accommodate the anticipated flow. As you open the internal systems to outside demands, you can't even guess what kind of load will develop.

Even after the system was up and running, changes had to be made on the fly, says Rubin-Stewart.

> We would find a bottleneck that was holding up the processing—maybe the engine, or the WebLogic server software itself, couldn't handle the volume. After we solved that problem, we would solve another engine, or database, problem. You might break one bottleneck, and then you didn't know what you would find when you opened the next set of doors. That was a really huge, eye-opening learning pro-

cess. I guess every company goes through that. It was very exciting.

Fixing all the bottlenecks wasn't easy, and required a lot of work, says Rubin-Stewart.

It was a combination of many things. We worked really closely with Datalex and also RTP, which had a lot of experience with these problems. It was a three-way group trying to do all this troubleshooting, because there were so many different places where things had to be fine-tuned. There were also things within the Datalex application that may not have been designed efficiently.

There were also changes to the front-end application. There was fine-tuning of the hardware it resided on, increase in the size of the hardware, fine-tuning of the engine itself, fine-tuning of the database, and fine-tuning of the servers. We went from one WebLogic server to five with a load balancer. Then there's the configuration—it changes when you have multiple servers. We had to double the capacity of our AS/400 servers. We didn't actually need to double it, we only needed to increase it by about 50 percent, but that's what IBM requires you to do. We also had to increase the size of the box that handled our management system. And then we had to address how all of these things communicated together.

White says being an early Web service adopter wasn't a risk, but a vital step that was required to ensure Vail's long-term success.

> The Internet is a very important component of not only booking travel, but travel in general. So it's a necessary part of every business at this point.

Enterprises need to view Web services in terms of bottom-line benefits, says White.

> Think about the revenue generation aspects of what you're doing. Try to tie things to an ROI. Change the use of online communications and e-commerce based on good business sense, not just trying to play follow the leader.
>
> Over the last five years, early in the onslaught of the Internet and the World Wide Web, there was a lot of an "everybody else has it, so I must need it, too" sort of mentality. Companies that are best at using the Internet have figured out specifically how it's going to improve their business online. They're the folks who have done those sorts of things, as opposed to just playing follow the leader.

Rubin-Stewart notes that Web services are becoming more of a mainstream technology, thanks to pioneers such as Vail. As a result of the work done by her company and other early adopters, IT managers have plenty to gain, and little to fear, from Web services.

> It's just like any development project. It all depends how cutting-edge you are, too. It will be much easier for someone else to use the Datalex engine, because it will be easier the second time around. I mean, when you look at it running in its end space, you kind of go: "Oh—this is very streamlined; it's very well de-

signed." But being in the development portion of this project, and developing a back end to it simultaneously, was very hard and very painful. It was well worth it, but it will be much easier for people the second time around, if they use applications that are already out there.

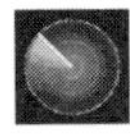

Chapter 5

Fairfax County, Virginia—Web Services in Government

Once a rural area dotted with farms, Fairfax County, Virginia, in the twenty-first century is a growing metropolis that hosts a thriving technology industry. Located in northern Virginia, near Washington, D.C., Fairfax County is home to many high-tech and government workers. The area also provides a variety of attractions, including over 300 parks, an impressive collection of eighteenth- and nineteenth-century landmarks, and Wolf Trap Farm Park for the Performing Arts, the only national park dedicated to the performing arts.

Fairfax County also has one of the largest concentrations of retail shopping on the East Coast. Tysons Corner Center and Tysons Galleria contain stores such as Bloomingdale's, Macy's, Saks Fifth Avenue, Lord & Taylor, and Nordstrom, as well as hundreds of upscale boutiques, specialty shops, and restaurants.

Meeting the governmental needs of Fairfax County's residents and businesses requires a substantial IT effort. Leading the infrastructure is Ray J. Herold, Fairfax County's director of technology architecture. Herold believes that Web services can be the key to making government more efficient and responsive to the needs of both people and business. Fairfax County has long been a leader in applying emerging technologies to governmental needs; it was one of the first government bodies in the world with its own Web site. Herold is currently working to bring Web services to any part of the county government's IT infrastructure that can benefit from the technology.

> We take pride in the fact that, even though we are a government entity, people perceive us as being forward-looking and a leader in the use of technology. We feel very strongly that technology offers us a way to provide more services to our citizens, hopefully at a reduced cost, and to provide services in a way that's more convenient.
>
> We have always tried to get our finger on the pulse of the industry, to see where things are going so that we can position ourselves not to the bleeding edge, but close to the edge. Close enough so that, when something looks really promising, we can be in a position to take advantage of the benefits that a particular technology might offer.

Web services first appeared on Herold's radar scope in the form of XML.

> We initially started looking at XML about two years ago and said, "Boy, this is really going to be a significant way for us to exchange information and not

> to have to worry about formats on the other end, the particular databases, and all of that.
>
> We started out looking at XML and kind of wound up looking at the SOAP, too. Extensible Markup Language is how you define the information, but Web services and SOAP provide the mechanism for actually delivering that information.

Herold appreciates the way Web services automate routine processes.

> Whether you're a government, or any kind of business, so much of what you do is really the same thing. Every time you build an application, you wind up reinventing that wheel each time. How many ways are there to post money to your accounting system? How many ways are there to register somebody for a particular service, or event?
>
> Prior to Web services, we were stuck in the situation of always having to reinvent the wheel. Web services changed that. We now have a way we can easily communicate with other levels of government. We can now make information available without bending over backwards, or changing our platforms or code. We now simply expose each particular business function as a Web service, register it in a Web Services Registry/Repository, and get access to these other jurisdictions, or even the public. We've extended our reach and our ability to provide information, without really having to do a whole lot of additional work on the functional side. As a result, we've seen a lot of benefits, both internally and externally.

Herold notes that something as simple, yet time-consuming, as address maintenance can greatly benefit from Web services.

> You can get databases from the postal service and several other places, but you've got to update them every so often. New addresses arise and zip codes change, so the database has to be upgraded on a regular basis, and that turns into an ongoing maintenance chore. If the postal service made zip code searches available as a Web service, then instead of getting a database and coding the database into your application, you could simply write a line of code that accesses the appropriate Web services. You wouldn't have to worry about updates and so forth, because you would be going directly to the source.

On a more serious level, Herold is currently planning a system that would use Web services to coordinate the processing of jail inmates.

> If we arrest somebody here, say for drunk driving or whatever, we want to make sure that person doesn't have a warrant someplace else. Or, if the person is currently in jail and we're getting ready to release him, we want to make sure he's not wanted anywhere else. Right now, there's really no single, easy way to do that. With the surrounding jurisdictions, we actually make telephone calls. It's not technologically sexy, and it's easy to miss something.

Web services would allow the various jurisdictions to coordinate their criminal justice activities with a minimum of human input, says Herold.

> Each jurisdiction has a list of people who are wanted—whether it's at the local, state, or even federal level. If we could all agree on a common schema for that information, through XML, then all of the jurisdictions could share data through a Web service. For example, if you had a person you were ready to release from jail, and his name, Social Security number, or other identifier comes up on the system, you could tell the jail: "Hold on, this person has a warrant." It would all be automatic and done in background through the exposure of functions that already exist for each jurisdiction.

Herold believes that Web services are destined to play an increasingly important role in government IT infrastructures.

> Probably 80 percent of the interaction that people have with government, at least as far as services go, is at the local level—police, fire department, human services, library, and so forth. But a lot of the programs are either funded, or in some way administered, at the state or federal level. Currently, there's no real way to pull all that information together for somebody who's trying to find out about a particular program, such as Section 8 housing. If you go to the county site, you get the county's perspective. If you go to the state site, you get its perspective. With Web services, we now have the ability to totally strip away those boundaries. For the citizen who's simply trying to get help, we can get information from all these layers, behind the scenes, then aggregate it and present it as a coherent block. Internally, Web services

> can offer a lot of benefits. Externally, however, we feel like the sky's the limit.

Fairfax County provides Web services externally through Recreation One-Stop. The initiative, managed by the U.S. Department of the Interior, is in the process of creating two products: the Recreation.gov (www.recreation.gov) Web site and the RecML data standard.

The Web site is designed to offer people single-point access to information about recreational opportunities nationwide. The service provides comprehensive information on approximately 2,500 public recreation sites. There are also plans to add thousands of additional facilities managed by state, tribal, and local governments. Additionally, Recreation.gov links to state tourism sites, providing information about thousands of private attractions and facilities.

Through Recreation.gov, people planning a trip will be able to:

- Discover which parks, forests, lakes, museums, and other recreation sites are located near a particular area.
- Sort through thousands of different recreation sites to find which ones offer specific recreational activities, such as hunting and camping.
- Find the location of recreation sites on maps, and obtain driving directions.
- Make reservations, order passes, and conduct other service transactions online.
- Link to related information and services provided by nongovernmental partners.

Thanks to the Internet and Web services, organizations can easily exchange data. But, in order to reduce potential confusion, it's also essential to be able to define specific language exchanged by partners. RecML will establish definitions for various recreation-related terms. RecML is being designed as a voluntary data standard that will be adopted by consensus within the recreation community to streamline the sharing of recreation-related data.

The RecML standard will define more terms than are displayed on the current Recreation.gov Web site. For example, Recreation.gov lists "fishing" as an activity, but a quick glance at the various state tourism sites will show that states advertise trout fishing, bass fishing, deep-sea fishing, and so on. The additional subcategories of fishing will be developed over the next few years, after a consensus is established among potential users.

The RecML standard will eventually be adopted officially by the Organization for the Advancement of Structured Information Standards (OASIS). The first version of RecML was scheduled to be drafted by September 30, 2003. Other versions will be developed in stages.

Fairfax County's participation in Recreation One-Stop goes back to a previous intragovernment Web services project called Government Without Boundaries (GWoB), a government-sponsored initiative that was eventually absorbed into Recreation One-Stop.

Lynn Hadden, Fairfax County's information architect, says that using Web services to feed data into Recreation.gov will make it easier for travel-related organizations to provide key information about Fairfax County activities to their users.

> Recreation.gov is the virtual repository, and Web services make the information available to others. Private, travel-related organizations, such as tour operators and travel agents, might want the same information on their Web site. They could have that information available for people who are traveling. That's the importance of using Web services.

Getting initiatives like Recreation One-Stop and GWoB off the ground required extensive cooperation among information providers, says Hadden.

> We had a large group dealing with the issue of managing intergovernmental collaboration. It was also a relatively diverse group. We had the State of New Jersey, the Commonwealth of Virginia, the General Services Administration (GSA), and many others.
>
> We all went through a lengthy process. We had to meet with the application people from each entity, decide exactly what data we needed to exchange, and what we were going to call that data in the schema. Then I came back here and mapped the schema to our SQL database. The Commonwealth of Virginia did the same thing, using the shared terminology that arose out of the schema. So, when we delivered the data, Recreation.gov knew the meaning of the data.

All of that hard work paid off by making it easier for Fairfax County to provide data to external organizations.

> Different groups request our data. In the past, formulating the data requested by a specific entity, and then populating their Web site, took quite some time to do. Now, by using Web services, a group can make a request whenever they want to, and get the exact data they need in the format that's required. There's no interaction between us—we just publish the Web service, and they go and use it. In other words, by generating the Web service, we can now point to it and say, "Our data is there, go get it." Before, people would want us to take our data, enter it into their systems, and update it in six different ways. That's not possible on a practical basis.

While technical coordination is important, business integration is a fundamental concern, says Hadden.

> The technology is not the problem—that's easy. The biggest obstacle to overcome is the business integration. That means getting people to understand why you're doing it and what you need to do to exchange the information. There has to be a real purpose for people to participate in these integrated activities, otherwise you can't sustain it.

Herold notes that as Fairfax County continues its commitment to Web services, his shop is focusing on Microsoft technology.

> We made the decision to do development on the .NET framework and the Microsoft series of components—Visual Studio .NET, .NET Server (now Windows Server), and ASP .NET. We think it provides a

good platform for Web services–oriented applications.

The choice we had to make was between .NET and J2EE. They both have their pluses and minuses—it really isn't a case where we think one is better than the other. We are already using Windows NT and Windows 2000 servers, MS Exchange, MS Windows desktop products, and IIS Web server. Our Web-based development is based on ASP, so .NET just became an extension of that. We already have a lot of experience with Microsoft platforms. We have people who know Visual Basic and ASP. We don't have too many people who know Java, so it really became a path of least resistance for us. Even so, we can see an environment in the future where we will have to support both platforms, and utilize the benefits they both provide as the opportunities present themselves.

Herold believes that the .NET platform provides enough Web services tools to provide a complete environment.

Microsoft .NET provides us with the kinds of things we're looking for (with the inclusion of SOAP and other necessary facilities) to provide a robust development platform. There is also a growing suite of third-party tools, which provide additional functionality and add-ons to the .NET environment.

Fairfax County is also using webMethods software to bring its legacy systems into the Web services loop.

> The webMethods software is an EAI—enterprise application integration product. It's also focused around XML and Web services.
>
> We're rewriting the Sheriff's system and, hopefully, that will be implemented in a couple of years. But a lot of our legacy systems are going to be around for a long while—seven, eight, nine, ten, eleven—maybe even twelve years. On older mainframe platforms, on older databases, and things like that, it's just not realistic for us to say, "We're going to go out and rewrite all these systems." That's because they're massive systems, and the resources just aren't there for us to do that.
>
> An EAI product (such as webMethods) gives us a way to access our old legacy systems, either at the database level, or at the transaction level. The software provides the information from different sources that must be aggregated, and then it either passes the data between the applications, or passes it on to users on an aggregate screen.

Herold likes the way webMethods gives Web services functionality to legacy systems with a minimum of tinkering.

> The great thing about webMethods is you don't really have to change your existing applications, since it's expensive to change code. What you can do, however, is change the application's functionality. You can integrate functionality, or parts of functionality, from different applications or different databases. You can actually end up with a whole that's greater than the sum of the parts.

> You can add more functionality to an application before it gets to the user through something like ASP. You actually have the ability not only to integrate your functionality, but to enhance it. With EAI products, such as webMethods, you can do that in a way that doesn't require you to go in and change your existing code. That's because webMethods has all of these different, built-in adapters.

Herold says he doesn't feel uneasy being an early Web services adopter. He believes that taking advantage of powerful new technologies is something of a duty.

> I feel very strongly that the nature of the IT profession has changed. You should always keep your eye out on what's over the horizon. That doesn't mean jumping over the cliff, but one also shouldn't get too comfortable in a particular niche. You'll get left behind and lose the opportunities that new technologies can provide. I think that's one of the reasons I'm in a management position. I've always been someone who feels strongly that you need to be conscious to what's coming along and to keep alert for things you might want to use in a particular environment. Yet, there's always risk in change, and you want to try to mitigate that risk.

Herold says he's proud to be associated with a forward-looking organization.

> The county has a reputation for being a leader in IT. We were among the first with a Web site. I'm personally very proud of that. We're probably ahead of most

> groups on the architecture level. We've worked, for example, with NASCIO—the National Association of State CIOs—in developing a flexible architectural framework that a lot of jurisdictions are just now starting to adopt.

It's important to lead an organization into well-researched risks, says Herold.

> Even if we wanted to be more conservative, we can't be. With all the high-tech companies in this area, people know what to expect from technology. They certainly talk to our elected officials and our county executive. Those people are aware of all kinds of things, and they're bound to ask us why we aren't doing certain things. We feel our trick is to stay one step ahead of them, or at least be ready to answer that question when they ask it.

Herold says IT managers shouldn't fear emerging technologies, such as Web services.

> You will, on occasion, misread the tea leaves. But I think there are some technologies that become so obvious that it almost becomes a no-brainer. Web services and XML fit into that category. I feel tremendously confident about this. It really is incumbent upon us to be positioned to utilize the benefits of new technologies for the benefit of the county's citizens. It's a way we can provide better services and more information.
>
> Whenever you're out front, there's always a little bit of concern. It's a calculation you do based on your

> experience, knowledge, and reading of where the industry is going. We talk to a lot of people, and we go to conferences. We're a client of Gartner [the Stamford, Connecticut–based technology research company], and we certainly get their advice before we take a plunge. In the case of Web services, I'm 100 percent convinced of their value. I would bet a year's salary. This is where it's all going.

Web services are just beginning to hit their stride, says Herold.

> I think there's still a bit of tweaking that needs to be done. But I also think that if you wait until the tweaking is done, you'll totally miss the boat.

Herold says he's looking forward to using additional Web services tools.

> I'm still sort of like a kid in a candy store, taking it all in, and thinking about all the stuff we can do. I would like to see a little more work done on the registries and repositories. That's how you make your services available to others, you put them in a registry/repository.
>
> It's roughly equivalent to a search engine, like Google, which is used to look for static information on the Web. It's sort of like that. You go to a registry/repository to find out what actual services, from a functional point of view, are available. You go through those and you think, "Oh, this is a good one. I want to use this in my application."

> The different industry sectors are working on XML vocabularies and registry/repositories. I know the chemical sector is working on one for their particular business area, the banks are working on one, insurance, manufacturing, and so on. A lot of the business sectors are working on this, but I'd like to see more work done on the government side. And I'd like to see more work on a higher level, not just the industry sectors doing it individually, but doing it on more of a universal kind of registry. To me, the one area where we're really not up to snuff yet is in the whole directory services area.

Herold offers prospective Web services adopters two bits of advice.

> The first word of wisdom is: Do look into it. The second is: Even if you're not willing to jump into it just yet, at least start doing things now to position yourself to be there, because this will happen, this is where [IT] is going.
>
> I've been doing [IT] for a long time, and there's only been a few things in my career where I've felt this confident about things. I've seen some really good technologies come and go. This is one of a small handful of those that I feel completely confident in. It's a relatively simple technology, but the benefits are humongous.

Chapter 6

Dow Jones & Company—From Ticker Tape to Web Services

Based in New York, Dow Jones & Company publishes a wide array of vital business and financial news and information. The firm's flagship publication, *The Wall Street Journal*, is the leading global newspaper of business. Dow Jones also publishes *Barron's*, a business and financial weekly; the *Far Eastern Economic Review*, a Hong Kong–based weekly magazine that provides current news and analysis on Asian business, economics, and politics; and *The Wall Street Journal Classroom Edition*, published monthly during the school year for U.S. high school students.

Dow Jones's position as the preeminent publisher of business and financial news and information extends well beyond the printed page. Many of the above titles are available on the Internet, including *The Wall Street Journal Online* (WSJ.com), the largest paid subscription site on the entire World Wide Web. Dow Jones also provides real-time news delivered electronically. The Dow Jones Newswires grew from the company's primary newswire, which has been the leading electronic provider of comprehensive business and stock market news to the securities industry for more than one hundred years.

Bill Godfrey is Dow Jones's CIO. Prior to joining the company in February 1999, Godfrey was senior vice president of IT services at insurance company Hartford Life. He was with Fleet Financial Group from 1989 to 1996, culminating with his position as senior vice president responsible for the bank's corporate cash management systems portfolio. From 1984 to 1989, Godfrey held a variety of positions supporting CIGNA's individual financial services division. Godfrey worked as a systems engineer for Electronic Data Systems from 1980 to 1984. He received a bachelor's degree from the University of Massachusetts, where he majored in finance.

As Dow Jones's CIO, Godfrey is constantly looking for ways to improve the company's information distribution efficiency and to cut costs. He feels that Web services fit the bill on both counts. Dow Jones recently began using Web services to automate the creation of the published financial statistics that are a company hallmark.

> In our market data area we use XML and Web services to automate a significant part of the tabular material that ultimately makes its way into our newspapers. The "C" section of *The Wall Street Journal* is virtually made up of scores of different categories of market data—equities, fixed income, currencies, charts, and analytics. We get data from the world's major financial exchanges. We also buy data from

> well over one hundred different sources—the Associated Press, Morningstar, Lipper, and so on. We bring that data into a content acquisition platform, a mechanism that takes in all the feeds and essentially puts them into a common format in a DJ–specific XML vocabulary. Web services is the glue that ties together approximately fifteen systems, written in different languages and on various platforms, that are necessary to create the different stats packages destined for the company's many publications.

Godfrey views Web services as an excellent way to boost efficiency and cut costs.

> Like a lot of companies, we've been going through excruciating cost pressures these last couple of years. At the same time, paradoxically, we've been making major investments in a business process redesign and increasing productivity. Over the past year, there's been quite a bit going on in *The Wall Street Journal*. We had a project called "Today's Journal." This initiative created the paper's new look and feel, including color on all the section fronts, a lot more color advertising capacity, the new Personal Journal section, and a redesigned market data section. If you look at the "C" section and see how that data is presented today versus a year and a half ago, it's quite different. It's the same with *Barron's*—a new look and feel; a new design.
>
> Our strategy for keeping up with the demands of the new product designs was to automate the creation of almost all of our stats. Because we're a media com-

> pany, all of our products are created every day, and they're consumed every day. It's what we call our "daily miracle." So everything's got a deadline, and we have to be able to do all this and meet the internal deadlines for all our products. The stat manipulation process is complicated and time-consuming. It requires a lot of people, and if we didn't automate it, we predicted we'd have deadline problems.
>
> Another important fact is that we're Dow Jones, which means we take quality and customer service incredibly seriously. Operationally, our processes are set up to double- and sometimes triple-check information to ensure accuracy and quality because that's part of our brand promise. So, in the market data world, people worldwide depend on *The Wall Street Journal* to be the authoritative source for market data. So we've had to be very careful as we automate that we protect the quality of the final product. I think we're off to a very good start on this.

Dow Jones decided to go with Microsoft technology.

> We're using Microsoft BizTalk as the Web services engine. A market data Extensible Markup Language taxonomy, leveraging SOAP, forms the application strategy that connects a bunch of product platforms and creates the final form market data and analytic packages that go into *The Wall Street Journal* and *Barron's*.

Godfrey was attracted to BizTalk by its price and capabilities.

It's a very well-priced platform. Also, my team felt that the administrative capabilities of the system, in terms of writing business rules and its work flow, were simple to understand and robust enough. And its basic XML management functionality was exactly what we wanted.

Prior to adopting Web services, Godfrey and his IT team brainstormed their way through an array of potential applications.

We prototyped for about a year, and created thirty or forty prototype Web services to make sure they could provide us with the capabilities we thought they could. So, we created things like a real-time quote service, a charting service, a "publish a piece of content" service, and a "publish a home page" service. We created a variety of prototypes so that we could determine if, in fact, Web services would live up to its billing.

Most of the applications worked as expected, says Godfrey.

We've got a half a dozen of these applets in place, but we were basically just dabbling, doing proof of concept work. The first real application was our market data automation project. That was number one. And that's principally where we use Web services today—in production.

Next on Dow Jones's Web services agenda is the automation of its Newswires, which transmit financial data and news to clients worldwide.

> We're in the process of redefining one of our core businesses: the real-time Dow Jones newswires. They're our most venerable business—110 years ago the information was provided on a ticker and printed on ticker tape.
>
> The Dow Jones newswires is a global electronic business that creates 5,000 to 10,000 stories every day, and pushes them out across a variety of networks. They go to the buy and sell sides of the professional finance community worldwide. There's domestic and international equity data, fixed income data, and capital markets data, as well as news stories on energy, commodities, and other topics. Basically, the Dow Jones newswires is a real-time financial services product that's provided to professional financial markets. It's news that moves markets.

Yet Dow Jones needs help in delivering its content to end users.

> This is a business where the vast majority of our content actually reaches our customers through third parties. So we push our content through Reuters, Bloomberg, and Thomson Financial, for example. They, in turn, provide terminals on our customers' desktops. These customers can be brokers, dealers, wealth managers, fixed income bond traders, and so on. We're in a marketplace that's consolidating into a few big players—Reuters, Bloomberg, Thomson, and a few other big houses. Yet the data has to reach hundreds of thousands of customers. One way to do that efficiently is to use Web services.

For content delivery, Web services provide a new level of convenience and efficiency, says Godfrey.

> The aim is to create technology capabilities that will allow us to integrate our news into work flows of our customers, while lowering the overall cost of product implementations and customer service administration. Traditionally, whenever a change was required, you would have to go onto your customers' premises, or work with them, have a programmer involved. That would be true every time you rolled out a new file format, or a new news feed. So, both for the customer and for Dow Jones, the traditional model required lots of business process integration, implementation, support, and coordination every time you wanted to make a change. We can avoid all that with Web services.

The first phase of Dow Jones's "Newswire of the Future" project is a service called Dow Jones NewsPlus. NewsPlus is also a new technology direction for Dow Jones. The first phase is a new Web site, and the XML–based feed is designed to give a convenient and interactive interface to the Newswires. Dow Jones's editors select and rank the most critical, market-moving stories for Dow Jones NewsPlus, with summaries on the home page and links to the complete story and related information such as press releases, industry news, and fundamental company data. The home page also provides stock and bond market updates, as well direct links to critical topics like politics and economic indicators. The interface also highlights select features, such as columns and analysts' comments.

It's designed to take what has traditionally been exclusively a proprietary, text-based, real-time, exchange format and move it to open industry standards. The way to do that is to evolve our news delivery using industry-standard Web techniques. That means embedding links within our content, so people can click through a story to get greater insight and analytics. It's designed to include analytics and to have more fielded data and richer meta data. It also offers a lot more personalized entitlement capabilities so that we can, on a finer level, give our downstream customers precisely what they want, allowing them to mix and match content. We want to be able to provide a delivery metaphor that allows customers to choose what content they want, and then how they want to display it. To do all of these things, we had to reinvent the way in which we distribute our content. Therefore, we're making some investments in emerging Web technologies, including Web-centric editorial platforms, XML taxonomies, and browser-based navigation.

What it comes down to is that we all want to personalize the desktop. And, if we want to tailor the data, the content, or the news to the specific requirements of that individual professional, then we need technologies that will enable that. The browser alone isn't enough. A fat client GUI can't do it. An old sort of model on a mainframe screen also can't do it. The idea in our business, in terms of real-time newswires, is to integrate news into the work flows of our customers. To do that, you need more than HTML. It just won't do it. You need more than XML. You need Web

> services. You need a public, well-understood, integration technology.

Dow Jones is also beginning to see many of its business partners and customers moving toward Web services.

> A lot of our partners, such as Thomson Financial, have embraced Web services as a strategy for application integration and B2B integration. Additionally, big customers like Merrill Lynch, Goldman Sachs, and Morgan Stanley are all beginning to use Web services as a B2B strategy, as well as an enterprise application integration strategy. Some of those companies are, in essence, technology companies—much more so than we are. We're a content company. We have a lot of technology capability and expertise that enables our products. But, at the end of the day, the core mission of my company is business news for businesspeople, not technology.
>
> However, when you move in to companies like Reuters, Thomson Financial, or Bloomberg, they can be considered technology companies. For example, at Thomson Financial, they have something like 2,500 employees in technology, because it's the nature of their business. Technology provides a competitive advantage, so companies like that are absolutely adopting Web services. I think that Web services have tremendous traction in these companies. So, if we want to integrate with CRM vendors, portals, or trading platforms, then we're going to need to adopt technologies that will make it much easier to do so. Otherwise, every customer is a one-off, and that's not good for either them or us.

> Web services is a technique that gives you flexibility to integrate applications on the desktop, to integrate applications over a wide area network, and to integrate applications over a local area network, using open industry standards. And it also leverages your investment in all your existing technologies. Web services really are a paradigm shift in that they make use of open industry standards. As a result, the network is already there. They can truly offer you a integration path that's easy to understand, easy to implement, and easy to support. I think it's a winner.

Web services is the ideal technology for CIOs facing the dual challenges of simplification and cutting costs, says Godfrey.

> Every CIO in America is facing the paradoxical challenge of cutting costs and raising productivity. One challenge is that we're all trying to simplify our infrastructure. We're all moving toward a portfolio orientation, and we're looking at our application inventory as a portfolio of assets. And we're all trying to figure out how to get more leverage out of that portfolio.
>
> CIOs are all trying to simplify, consolidate, and rationalize. In the old days, you would maybe mount one of these big "boil the ocean projects." You know, doing CRM across the company, supply chain management, or enterprise application integration. Everything was enterprise-level with a big "E." They became very difficult projects. A better technique today is continuous improvement with the point of view in mind that says: Integrate and consolidate

where you can prove there is incremental value to the company.

With Web services, you don't suffer the big productivity hit that the "boil the ocean projects" create. At the same time, you can accomplish the goal of simplification. I think all CIOs are looking for a simplification dividend. The dividend comes from lowering your costs and reducing your operational headaches. Because Web services are at a sufficiently high level of abstraction, you can leverage existing technologies; they sit on top of legacy. The power is in having a standard way to investigate.

When it comes to a content-driven company like Dow Jones, Web services allow easier content reuse, notes Godfrey.

I've got multiple systems to create *The Wall Street Journal* and the real-time Dow Jones newswires. As I share and repurpose content, everything is done through black boxes—-file handlers. The format coming out of *The Wall Street Journal* publishing systems is not compatible with Dow Jones newswires, so I have to write code. The format of the copy coming out of *Barron's*, which ultimately goes to WSJ .com, also isn't in the right format, so I have to write code.

Part of my competitive advantage at Dow Jones is tied to how well I can reuse content and tailor it to the medium in which it's ultimately expressed. Today, that takes programmers and big projects. With a Web services approach, I can make the repur-

> posing and the reuse of content a simpler, and less expensive, process.

Godfrey notes that the mere mention of Web services tends to raise unnecessary apprehensions in some CIOs.

> My belief is that Web services, as a programming technique, aren't particularly difficult. They represent nowhere near the paradigm shift that was presented by second-, third-, or fourth-generation languages. They're relatively straightforward. I believe you can get your feet wet with Web services without a lot of risk. You can use them as an interapplication integration technique. That, I think, offers a lot of benefits right away. Using Web services as a means to build up a repository of reusable components, however, represents another level of maturity. That can be harder to tackle. Like object-oriented development in the 1980s, will the company stay the course long enough to actually create enough objects to make the investment worthwhile? It's not a strategy you want to go halfway with.

Still, Godfrey believes that Web services' potential for providing inexpensive, reusable components is strong.

> The idea of reusable components and methods and object-oriented technology has been around for quite some time. Earlier attempts failed because they were swept away by new technologies, because the development skills were hard to come by, or simply because they weren't very good. One also had to

> wait a long time and build up enough components to make the effort worthwhile, and many people lost the will to wait that long.
>
> For example, I was part of a Smalltalk team years ago when I worked in the insurance industry. We had built up hundreds and hundreds of objects, using Smalltalk for an insurance claim system. But the process just took too long—several years. Management lost patience with the fact that it took so long, and it was so darn expensive. And, at the end of the day, it was still proprietary. So we killed the project.
>
> Web services are different, though. With Web services, you don't have to rewrite all the functional code. While some services will have to be written from scratch, many will be reusing capabilities you already have. That's how it's different from older models, which had to be fit to proprietary languages like Smalltalk, or proprietary frameworks, like CORBA.

Dow Jones's Web services platform marks a major change from the company's previous technology.

> We didn't have a framework; we were, primarily, a C++ application shop with applications running on top of a variety of Sun boxes and an IBM mainframe. There were some COBOL applications on the mainframe and close to a dozen C++ apps running on top of the Sun boxes.

The use of middleware remains an unsolved problem for Godfrey.

> We have NQ Series in some of our application portfolios, but we don't yet have a standard middleware platform across all applications. That's going to be a part of our next generation work.
>
> We kind of look at Web services as a stand-alone topic, but it's actually integrated to the middleware in an N-tiered distributive model. We are continuing to build N-tier distributive applications. That's a given. A very small portion of our portfolio uses third-party middleware—in the past, we usually rolled our own. Going forward, we'll begin to use even more third-party middleware. That's being evaluated.

On the whole, Godfrey has found few drawbacks to Web services.

> There were some implications where performance was considered an issue. There's some overhead with Web services, with XML and SOAP. The XML vocabularies themselves, for example, are bulky. There's something like a two-times or three-times increase in characters transmitted. You need to be careful of that. So there was some concern, when we did our proof of concept, that Web services may not fit every usage profile.

Godfrey is particularly concerned about the suitability of Web services in a real-time environment.

> Anyone who's engaged in real-time data management ought to figure out for himself if Web services make good sense. I think, ultimately, they will. But the nature of a real-time environment is that it's real

time. People are paying a premium for a real-time application, and the quality, authenticity, and authority of the data are all important.

In real time, the publishing systems are typically built differently. The error recovery, tagging, coding, and indexing are all important. It's just a different paradigm. So, as we move to Web services for all the reasons we talked about, we should make sure that we don't have a service-level issue in real-time applications.

Another area of concern for Godfrey is XML.

There are a lot of people who can create XML, but it's often not well formed or well thought-out. You've got to be careful of that. I think it's very much like creating a schema for a relational database. You need people who are really good at information management and information models, which is not a technology problem per se. It's a matter of getting technology to relate at various levels of abstraction data to make sure that the XML implementation will actually work and also provide scalability. That's the issue. You can hard-code anything, but, during the day, you want to make sure that it's leverageable, extensible, and scalable. That only comes about if someone really smart thinks through the information model in such a way that it is scalable.

This goes back twenty years to how people would argue about normalization techniques. It's a little bit of the same thing now: How do you approach creating your information models? Is it a good fit for the

> problem that needs to be solved? That's something I don't know; I can't give you the definitive answer. But it's something I'd be a bit wary of—that you don't apply Web services to every problem. You still have to think through and ask what the right technique is for a particular problem.

Godfrey also has concerns about third-party UDDI services.

> I'm certainly not going to be a market leader in that regard. I do think the UDDI concept makes good sense. I suspect for a period of time I'll provide my own UDDI directory. I wouldn't use a third party, but in the future I might, if it was a trusted third party, and if there were enough applets and components that it would really speed my development.
>
> I'm not particularly worried about security, and I'm not particularly worried about the flexibilities of WSDL. I'm not particularly concerned with semantic applications—I think there's plenty of robustness in the protocols and the framework.

Godfrey believes that the excitement that Web services have generated is mostly justified.

> Web services have provoked some new thinking for me. As a CIO, the debates and dialogues about Web services have resonated with me more than other enterprise application strategies. So, I'm more interested in Web services than I have been interested in some of the predecessor technologies and ap-

> proaches. The idea of a services-oriented architecture is very appealing to me.

The Web services bottom line, says Godfrey, is the bottom line.

> In the financial services space, Web services are getting a lot of traction. So Dow Jones has to keep up. It's our intention to use Web services to add value and to lower costs.

Chapter 7

Regular Baptist Press—Web Services in Publishing

Based in Schaumburg, Illinois, Regular Baptist Press is the publishing arm of the General Association of Regular Baptist Churches (GARBC). The organization publishes Sunday School curriculum and a wide array of religiously themed books, including titles on Bible studies, Christian living, and church administration. The organization also publishes a variety of classroom and home study textbooks.

David Bosket is Regular Baptist Press's director of technology. Bosket is looking to Web services to provide the automatic integration of product, customer, and inventory information. He notes that Regular Baptist Press entered into Web services when it began revamping its direct sales Web site.

> About 15 percent to 20 percent of our business is done through the Web. Previously, we had a CGI–, Perl-based environment that had very limited functionality. We had to hard-code everything. If this

> month we entered a customer's credit card number, shipping address, and billing address, and the customer returned with another order the next month, we would have to repeat exactly the same process. It was a huge inconvenience for our customers and internal support staff. So, we decided to take a look at developing a more comprehensive Web site—one that could retain customer information and instantly recognize customers whenever they come back.

Bosket's first step in creating such a system was to utilize S3-CISPUB, a publishing industry–oriented ERP product.

> We acquired S3-CISPUB, which has an e-commerce interface that imports records and text-based files, which got my mind going. I thought, if it can be done manually, why couldn't the process also be accomplished automatically?

Bosket's next step was to find a Web-based technology that would tie product, customer, and inventory information into one neat package. While attending an S3-CISPUB user group conference, Bosket met Mary Westheimer, founder and chairman of BookZone, a Scottsdale, Arizona–based company that designs e-commerce Web sites for book publishers. Bosket says BookZone offered technology that appeared to closely match his need for automatic data integration.

> We started talking about what it would take to develop a Web site that was fully integrated and could automatically and directly dump records from our

> Web store right into an order-entry system and vice versa. Such a system, rather than requiring manual inputs or imports, would just automatically supply the data wherever it was needed. It would also allow discount structures to be put in place and provide customer recognition capabilities and several other sophisticated operations.

The Web environment that Bosket, Westheimer, and S3-CISPUB cocreated consists of four main components. The primary Web store functionalities are provided by BookZone; however, the product and customer content management is supported and maintained by S3:

1. CISPUB—The Regular Baptist Press's ERP system. The system includes:
   - The centralized data components, such as product information, customer accounts, and tracking information, are entered, maintained, and updated within CISPUB.
   - A text file is passed to BookZone twice daily with these records updated to provide current and relevant information to our Regular Baptist Press customers.

   All credit card processing will be accomplished on CISPUB to help maintain consistency in record keeping.
2. BZGenesis—The Regular Baptist Press's Web site. The site includes:
   - A database-generated catalog.
   - A search engine.
   - A shopping cart and other e-commerce capabilities.

- Secure ordering.
- An FTP gateway.
- E-mail capabilities.

3. BZHarmony—The middleware that lies between S3-CISPUB and BZGenesis. It includes:
   - Support for Web site order entries.
   - A secure FTP gateway for information exchange.
   - Fully automated product database system integration. (The software updates the Web site's product database with S3-CISPUB's current product database on a scheduled basis.)
   - An integrated product inventory that displays the current quantity of products available and the status of products that are currently unavailable.
   - Customer information support, including the autopopulation of fields in the shopping cart system and order tracking.
4. BZHub—BookZone's hosting service, which uses a Windows 2000 server platform and point-to-point T1 access.

The environment's BZHarmony middleware contains the core Web services components. BZHarmony was developed with ColdFusion, a Macromedia product. Compatible with J2EE application servers, ColdFusion is designed to allow Web application developers to utilize a Java-oriented Web services strategy.

Westheimer says it was important for the Regular Baptist Press to have a middleware product that could allow a seamless and flawless exchange of information, utilizing XML and other Web services technologies.

> BZHarmony's bidirectional implementation is a bit like a post office drop. We take information gathered at the Web site, drop it to a database, and then transfer it to CISPUB, where the information is imported and verified.

The overall Web site brings a high degree of integration to Regular Baptist Press's Web site and back-end operations, says Westheimer.

> Among the functions are order status, order history, order tracking, inventory updates, and product updates. It's all bidirectional, so any changes made in the business system are transferred to the site. That reduces errors and increases correlation and accuracy.

Westheimer believes that Web services are becoming a cost-effective tool. She notes that the technology is rapidly replacing custom-built and proprietary information exchange technologies.

> It's really a sound vision, because of the cost-effectiveness and the fact that we're now able to feed through all sorts of different information. Extensible Markup Language has been a big part of that, replacing technologies that people in our industry have been paying a considerable amount of money for. The Web enables us to increase the speed and lower costs, and that's very important.

Westheimer feels that Web services are ushering in a new era of Web-centric businesses.

> The concept is to utilize the Web as the center of an organization's IT operations. I have been gratified to find that, when I offer this message to the publishing industry, I get a great response. Five years ago, they would have rolled their eyes politely, because the vision hadn't yet been widely accepted and also because the technology wasn't where it is now.
>
> The Web was, for a long time, a big question mark. There was a tendency to set up operations separately. In other words, we have a Web site over here and business intelligence and CRM systems over there; we have our business system over here and our warehouse management operations system over there. That's where Web services come in; they get all the operations to mesh together.

By providing robust integration functions, Web services have the potential to eliminate repetitive, time-wasting activities, says Westheimer.

> In the past, organizations would find themselves inputting the same data in three or four different places. That's a waste of resources, of course. So the Regular Baptist Press's project shows real foresight. Bosket's ideas, meshed with BookZone's and S3's technology, allows information to be entered just once, and then shared throughout the system.

Westheimer notes that Web services provide a substantial improvement in resource management, although many enterprises are unaware of this, or simply fail to recognize this fact.

> I give the Regular Baptist Press a lot of credit for seeing this fact so clearly and embracing it. I think a lot of this vision has to do with David Bosket himself and his ability to see the big picture clearly. It's very impressive.

Bosket says he tapped BookZone because of his own limited development resources.

> My IT team consists of only two people: an application developer and a system administrator. I only have one programmer, who also has other responsibilities. Utilizing my application developer to tie everything together and to accomplish everything in-house would have been unacceptably costly, and it would have taken a very long time. I didn't want to tie up my resources. Going to BookZone was much more cost-efficient than trying to do it ourselves.

Bosket says he was never very concerned about being an early Web services adopter.

> I've never been concerned about that. To me, the technology is mature enough that it's not an issue. Everything may not run right away, but that's to be expected with any new deployment. I really feel that Web services' maturity, at least as far as database integrations go, is mature enough.

While Web services are often associated with cutting-edge, start-up businesses, Bosket notes that the technology is also critical to established enterprises.

> We're a traditional business that's been in operation for over fifty years. Yet we need to keep up with the market and new marketing channels, such as the Web. We would go out of business if we looked at things from a traditional perspective. We must keep in tune with our customers and have the correct feel for meeting their needs.
>
> It is the marrying of the technology to tradition that I see going on right now. People are no longer trying to create bubbles of utopia and wonderment; they're trying to conduct a business. We need to tie technology into our traditional business model. I need to have cost factors and ROIs, just as in a traditional business model.
>
> We are currently in the testing phase of this project. We have had a number of issues come up, such as data manipulation and scrubbing, and normal testing glitches. However, each issue that has arisen has been dealt with, with a systematic and methodical approach, and eventually taken care of.

So far, the deployment has gone rather smoothly, says Bosket.

> As far as obstacles go, I haven't had any major problems. I'm anticipating a few, minor glitches during this first year of operation, but I'm not really anticipating any huge problems. Maybe I'm looking at things

> through my rose-colored glasses, but I'm not anticipating anything big.

Despite the overwhelming hype surrounding Web services, Bosket says he tries to take a pragmatic view of the technology's capabilities.

> I want to use Web services to enhance our organization's ability to perform sound business functions. That's really what the technology is there for. Something like Web services is not meant to do everything—it's not designed to replace people, for example. The technology is simply there to help your business processes perform in a better way.

Bosket notes that it's important to keep open to new ideas and to maintain clear and open communication channels.

> Communication is very important. You have to know your business, and you have to be willing to communicate with your people to know what's going to work and what's not going to work. There must be support from the top down. You need to know what the workers in the trenches are doing.
>
> One also needs to have a solid understanding of technical and business processes. If you sit back and think, "Well, it should work this way," and you don't really know for sure, you're going to get burned. We've been hit a couple of times—in minor ways—by that kind of mind-set. Sometimes, you just

> don't know how processes and technologies will work. Guessing at things isn't a good approach to follow. Nothing beats practical knowledge.

An IT manager developing a Web services project also needs to be able to distribute responsibility. It's important to involve both internal employees and external consultants in key project aspects, says Bosket.

> One of the things we struggled with a little bit was delegating responsibility. In other words, exactly who is responsible for a particular area? A couple times, when dealing with BookZone, I felt like telling their people, "You know your system, tell me what I need to put in there." Their response would be, "But this is dealing with your business process, so you tell us what you want it to be." There was this nebulous gray area between us. At times, it really did feel like "us" versus "them."

BookZone's Westheimer says team meetings, held during the development process, allowed Regular Baptist Press's managers to air concerns and set responsibilities.

> We got everybody on a conference call; all the people who would be involved with the site's functions—marketing, business management, and IT. Everybody talked things through in terms of what they would like to have, what was important to them, and what they never wanted to have happen to them.
>
> Having such a meeting is powerful, because it allowed us to get information from the departments

that are on the front lines. These people experience things, see things, and know things that management may not be aware of, and probably shouldn't be, because they have other concerns. These are the nitty-gritty, nuts-and-bolts details that only the people in the trenches know. One gets a much better design result from their input.

From a management standpoint, this sort of session provides a really good buy-in. Otherwise, the managers are simply having something done to them. By airing their views and listening to the various reactions, they're participants. They're on the team. The approach allows them to understand what's being done and why it's happening. They're now a part of the process, and they have an investment in getting everything working and going forward.

Bosket says the cooperation between Regular Baptist Press managers and BookZone and S3 representatives benefited all organizations.

Ultimately, we worked through things and we were able to get what we needed.

With a rapidly changing technology, like Web services, it's important to have the ability to learn quickly, says Bosket.

I'm discovering all this stuff by trial and fire. It took a lot of time to learn all the processes and to be able to communicate with people.

The learning process is very important. When we went into this project, five of our top people had been in their jobs for less than a year. We all had to make a major conversion. Thankfully, we were blessed that everything has fallen into place. We've learned a lot. We all hung in there.

Chapter 8

Eric Scott Custom Products—Web Services with Style

Eric Scott Custom Products is a company that's eager to change with the times. Until just a couple of years ago, the St. Genevieve, Missouri–based firm focused on manufacturing high-quality personal leather goods and molded business accessories. Today, Eric Scott is less of a leather manufacturer and more of a business solutions provider, offering its clients a diverse array of manufactured products, design development, importing, fulfillment, and automation services.

Eric Scott has a well-deserved reputation as an innovator. In the mid-1990s, for example, the company abandoned its traditional assembly-line approach and switched to cellular manufacturing. The method calls for teams operating in cells of four to eight people, working on projects that may require many dozens of steps to complete. Team members are cross-trained, rotate jobs frequently, and take ownership of the completed product. Today, as it continues to shift toward new products and services, Eric Scott is blazing a technology trail in Web services.

Joe Young, Eric Scott's director of information systems, says Web services technology allows the company to communicate with customers and vendors more efficiently and effectively.

> The Web services tie directly to supply chain management. With our customer-focus strategy, we need to be able to provision critical information, such as shipping dates, delivery dates, shipping methods, package locations, and so on. Being able to provision that through the Web on a 24/7 basis has really become critical for the operation.

To reach his goal, Young turned to software from Made-2Manage, an Indianapolis-based business software vendor. Eric Scott uses the Made2Manage Enterprise Business System, which includes M2M ERP, an enterprise resource planning product; M2M VIP, an enterprise portal; and M2M Link, a Web services connectivity product that features the Web services support provided by the Microsoft .NET Framework. EDI, XML, and flat-file communications are supported.

The M2M VIP portal relies on XML and SOAP to provide Web-enabled communications services. M2M VIP offers access to critical back-end information and processes, giving customers and vendors immediate self-service capabilities. With M2M VIP, there's no need to rewrite back-office applications, or maintain duplicate sets of data. The technology provides secure

Web browser–based access to anyone, anywhere, at any time.

> We have the Made2Manage Enterprise Business System as our back-end ERP system. We also have a Web front end that information is provisioned through. So, on the distribution side, if we ship an order at 11:00 A.M., for example, and someone wants to learn about that order's status at 11:05 A.M., she can log on through a simple Internet connection and visit our Web site to see if the order has shipped. The system provides a connection to UPS WorldShip that makes it possible for customers to place and track orders from beginning to end.

Nearly all customer and supplier communications can now be accomplished through the Web site, says Young.

> They go to our portal. Inputting a secure user name and password gives access to a specific Web page for each company and user. They can then click on the order section, look at a particular sales order, and find out whether or not it's been shipped. They can also take the UPS tracking number, which is populated in the system, and connect to UPS World-Ship, pop it in there, and track their package. Users don't have to place a phone call to a customer service representative, send an e-mail, or wait for information—they just go to the Web site and view whatever they need to know.

The system also allows Eric Scott to accept customer orders. The orders can come in via EDI. Once placed, the orders are scheduled for manufacturing and shipment. All critical information is made available to customers via the portal in real time.

> Orders can be placed through M2M VIP, using either our part number or the customer's own part number. Because each item is identified to a specific customer, a user only has access and can only order items that are specific to his operation.
>
> Thanks to the excellent administrative tools built into M2M VIP, we can pick and choose what users get to see on their menus. To us, this flexibility is vital. As everyone knows, no two companies are the same, and different users within organizations have various needs. This goes hand in hand with our customer-focused strategy.

M2M VIP has proven to be a crucial element in Eric Scott's Web services infrastructure, says Young.

> We see it as a kind of all-functioning, universal portal that lets us offer our customers just about any service they need. M2M VIP has a simple, clean, Web-based interface. But the beauty of this offering is the back-office integration. Certainly, for manufacturers there's a high cost to develop this kind of back-office integration. Made2Manage has written this piece, which is really what makes M2M VIP shine.

The system also supports a variety of data exchange formats beyond EDI.

> Most of the businesses we deal with provide us information in many forms other than EDI. We didn't want to leave any customers or vendors out of the picture. Supply chain management and vendor-managed inventory capabilities were some of the issues we considered early in the design process.
>
> Our system allows us to tell a vendor, "We need X amount of feet of leather in this color immediately." That vendor can then come in and say, "This is how much this supplier has on order with us, and this is where they've got it scheduled to be delivered." The vendor can even give us more detail, such as, "It looks like the supplier is running a little low, so perhaps we should confirm the order and maybe go ahead and make a shipment ahead of schedule." All of this puts more eyes on the situation; it gets everybody into the ball game.

M2M VIP also provides document-sharing and collaboration capabilities. The software allows Eric Scott to exchange "virtual design" documents with customers, enabling them to easily review and reuse past designs. The software also provides a record of design development, including which alterations were made when and by whom.

> We have a document repository in which we can place just about any kind of document. The repository has areas that are specific to each customer. We can share Excel documents, Word documents, CAD files, and a variety of other materials.

Tracking functions and other management features help Eric Scott managers and customers keep firm control over various documents.

> If we put an Excel file out there, for example, we can initiate several types of actions from that file. Any time a change is made to the document, an e-mail can be automatically sent out to notify all of the file's users. The document is also associated with discussion threads and an online history. Files can also be posted as read-only documents to prevent accidental changes. Different user access levels are managed from the administrative side, so there's always full control over the environment.

The system replaced a patchwork of older technologies.

> While we still use EDI, conventional e-mail, faxing, and phone calls—the traditional methods of conducting business—Web services are enhancing our company and our customer and vendor relationships.

A service server supplies the connection between Eric Scott's systems and the Internet, says Young.

> The link is SSL–encrypted at 128 bits. There's a .NET infrastructure, using SOAP and XML, that talks to our back-office system and transitions the information from our back-end system through our server and back to the vendor or customer—whoever is calling for information from the Web.

Young recognized the potential of Web-based communications long before the technology went mainstream.

> As far back as 1997, we knew that was where things were headed.

The increasingly global nature of Eric Scott's business was a prime motivator for adopting Web services, says Young.

> If we're dealing with somebody who's on the other side of the world, it's a simple fact that we're not in the office when they're in their office. So, in the past, we had to work exclusively by fax exchanges or play phone tag. The portal effectively solves that problem.

Eric Scott's Web services system was created to handle everyday business needs, says Young.

> Our primary focus was to create a very solid infrastructure that could run the business day in and day out and provide everyone internally with the resources they needed to have. Secondarily, we needed to make sure that we could implement the Web services when the time was right. So, that's what we really looked at and implemented.
>
> We evaluated about a dozen different packages during late 1998 and early 1999. In June 1999, we settled on the Made2Manage solution. One of the edges they had was covering over 80 percent of our total needs. We really didn't want to build a lot of customizations internally.

Made2Manage provided the development support that helped Young see concepts unique to Eric Scott become reality. As it turned out, many of the features they needed were already built into the system.

> We were able to give a tremendous amount of input as to what we needed from the system, what it would contain, and the functionality it would provide. Made-2Manage paid attention. They listened to us with an open mind. For us, that's the way the system was developed and rolled out.

The vendor brought Young and his team into the software design process.

> I actually got to speak with a lot of the folks who were developing Made2Manage's Web services. They didn't have them yet, but they were coming shortly. Made2Manage followed through on everything they said they would provide.
>
> We implemented the accounting side of the ERP system in October 1999, and then we turned the rest of the system on in January 2000. We went cold turkey; we didn't run dual systems. For our particular situation, we decided that we had to look at the logistics of keeping up with two different systems and how practical that was going to be. For us, it was not going to be practical. So, we ran just the new Made2-Manage system, and I can honestly sit here today and say, we really had no significant issues.

Young feels that the key to a successful Web service implementation lies in careful planning.

> Planning and execution is critical. If the planning is done well, and the plan executed with dedication, the rest of the puzzle tends to take care of itself. Then, if a few snags do show up, you won't find yourself putting out so many fires that it becomes overwhelming.

Once the planning was completed, system deployment went very quickly, says Young.

> There were a few kinks to work out. But, for the most part, it only took us about a week or two to get everything in place. That's in spite of the fact that we were still working out the system's logistics. That was a few years ago, in the early days. Today, it only takes a matter of hours to implement the M2M VIP services. It takes hardware at our site, for example, to actually run the Internet information server. As a result, there was a lot of logistics juggling involved in the rollout—a lot of things that had to be worked out. This is normal when you are a beta tester or early adopter. But we were actually pleasantly surprised that everything went so smoothly.

Young believes that the greatest resistance to Web services comes from the unrealistic promises of software vendors.

> A lot of people are still leery of Web services. Expectations are really pumped, and they're disappointed

> when a product fails to live up to its unrealistic promise. I think that leaves a bad taste for a while.
>
> That's where our relationship with Made2Manage succeeded then and continues to succeed today. They provided exactly what was promised. They're also continuing to support the technology and are helping it to evolve and grow. This has been a major effort on their part.

Young says he had some fears about being an early Web services adopter. Most of his concerns, however, revolved around potential time constraints, not the technology itself.

> You always have concerns, because it's something that's going to take a chunk of time from your internal IT staff. Since we have a pretty small staff, shifting to a new technology can really have an impact on daily operations. If you're spending a lot of time on this, then you don't have the ability to cover other important bases. That was our concern. On the other hand, we've never been unduly fearful of time demands, because if it takes a Saturday or Sunday to get the job done, we do it.

But Young says his fears began to fade away shortly after deployment.

> Our fears were silenced after the first couple of days, because that's when a lot of the catastrophic sorts of things that could happen—like trying to run something and it toasts your server or corrupts your data-

> base—would likely occur. Those sorts of things never happened, however. One always has to have some kind of contingency planning against the worst-case scenarios. We did that. But, fortunately, we didn't have to use those plans.

Young believes that Web services are destined to become a key and virtually universal business technology in the very near future.

> There are still people who have to be convinced, but the trend toward Web-based communications is growing. It's actually invading some of the old standards, like EDI. For now, though, we're supporting EDI, XML, and other technologies through our portal.

Looking into the future, Young says he's eagerly anticipating new Web services technologies.

> We're always looking at ways that we can better serve our customers. One of the things we'll definitely be looking at is continuously implementing the newer kinds of technology. There's nothing wrong with the older versions, but we just believe developing the newer technologies will make for a smoother transition and a better overall integrated operating platform.
>
> We're always looking for ways to give information to whoever needs it—whoever is in contact with our business. We're always taking a look at that and evaluating what we need to incorporate.

Like many early Web services adopters, Young believes that the technology is beneficial. Yet putting a finger on a precise ROI is difficult, since most of the benefits are in the hard-to-measure areas of productivity and customer satisfaction.

> I don't have any figures, but I do know that the number of phone calls we receive has been greatly reduced. That's because answers can now be obtained through the Web. We've been able to utilize staff in other areas, just because we don't have to personally answer every single question for our customers.
>
> We love talking to customers and vendors, but we don't want them to be forced into a situation where they have to call us or e-mail us just to get some information. Additionally, there's the flexibility. If a customer has a question at 5:00 P.M. on a Saturday and the information is attainable via the Web, he simply goes and gets it. He doesn't have to wait until Monday for an answer. There's also an enhanced return to our vendors, thanks to our adoption of vendor-managed inventory. We want to make it easier for them and easier for us. It's hard to put a value on all of that.

Young offers some final words of advice.

> I take the same approach to Web services that I do with any sort of business situation: Don't rush in and jump off the deep end without doing some homework. It's worth the time and the effort to go and learn about Web services. Once that investment in time

has been made, the true worth of the system can be evaluated. If the technology fits a need, a better plan can be constructed, offering a better opportunity for a successful implementation.

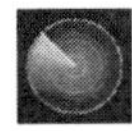

Chapter 9

Agfa HealthCare—A Web Services Cure

Agfa HealthCare, a subsidiary of Mortsel, Belgium–based Agfa-Gevaert Group, specializes in analog and digital imaging solutions, as well as a variety of diagnostic and communications systems. With its U.S. headquarters located in Greenville, South Carolina, Agfa HealthCare supplies computer-based radiography and digital networks for hospitals. The company's equipment, consumables, and services are targeted to different hospital departments and comprise comprehensive information systems tailored to the needs of the hospital.

Christine Vincent is Agfa HealthCare's global e-business director. Prior to joining the company, Vincent was global IT director for Sterling Diagnostic Imaging, a manufacturer of medical imaging film, film processing equipment, and electronic imaging systems and services. Vincent arrived at Agfa HealthCare after Sterling was acquired by Agfa in June 1999.

Agfa HealthCare began looking into Web services technology when its largest customers started asking the company to participate in a B2B Internet exchange.

> We decided to answer the expectation of our main customers. They wanted us to participate in an exchange marketplace, so we looked at the software packages that would ease the integration of the collaboration between our ERP system, which is SAP, and the exchange marketplace, which, at that time, was Medibuy.
>
> Medibuy has since been acquired by Global Healthcare Exchange (located in Westminster, Colorado), and we are now in the process of transitioning from Medibuy to GHX. This has created some delays and slowed the adoption rate for all the parties involved. We are far from reaching the critical mass we are aiming for, unfortunately, but the volume growth is steady and significant.
>
> So far, we're working with about fifty customers. Our goal is a few hundred within two years. The number of dealers, distributors, and OEMs we're connected with is four. We ultimately plan to connect with fifteen. Sales handled through the exchange are currently less than one percent of our overall revenue, but the figure is growing exponentially each month.
>
> Group purchasing organizations (hospitals that have joined into a purchasing alliance), OEMs, and larger distributors also require us to do our business electronically. They want us to be ready for the next e-commerce wave. The unique aspect the health-care model presents is that a lot of GPOs put pressure on

> their suppliers to participate in an exchange marketplace, so they can have better visibility of what's being purchased by their member hospitals.

Vincent turned to Comergent Technologies to supply the Web tools Agfa HealthCare needed to participate in the exchange.

> Comergent was picked as the result of my research into other industries, such as high-tech and telecom. I looked at Cisco as the model, and Cisco used Comergent. So I talked to Cisco about the functions they use and discovered that it would be easy to adapt them to the health-care market.

Agfa HealthCare is using the Comergent E-Business System (specifically, a subset of applications formerly marketed under the name "Private Marketplace Suite") and Comergent Network Service, including these following modules:

C3 Profile Manager

C3 Product Manager

C3 MarketLink

C3 Partner.com

C3 Advisor

C3 Analyzer

> The main Web service we provide is a continuous flow from the purchase acquisition at a hospital

> through an exchange marketplace to a distributor, a dealer, or an OEM partner, not losing the direct ownership of the transaction, as well as the visibility of the transaction having real-time, online information, based on whatever is transacting between the hospital and the distributor, the dealer, or OEM. We have a closed-loop process in place, fully tested from requisition to purchase order, followed by order acknowledgment, then physical delivery, and electronic invoicing with the possibility of electronic fund transfer for payment.

Here's a basic view, in five steps, of how Agfa Health-Care's system works:

1. *A purchase order is sent from the hospital or GPO via the exchange to an Agfa Healthcare dealer, distributor, or OEM.* The dealer, distributor, or OEM is chosen based on the stated preference of the purchasing hospital or GPO. An electronic copy of the purchase order is sent to Agfa Healthcare.
2. *The dealer, distributor, or OEM responds by sending an order acknowledgement back to the hospital, validating the product's pricing and availability.* An electronic copy of the order acknowledgment is sent to Agfa Healthcare.
3. *The order is shipped.*
4. *An invoice is generated.* If the order involves a large dealer, distributor, or OEM, the seller creates an invoice in its own back-office system and then links into the Comergent platform to send electronic cop-

ies, via the exchange, to both Agfa HealthCare and the hospital or GPO that made the purchase. If the order involves a small dealer, distributor, or OEM, the seller creates an invoice using the Partner.com module. This allows the company to access the Comergent system via a standard Web browser without the more complex integration to a back-end system. The selling company then uses the Comergent platform to electronically send, via the exchange, the invoice to both Agfa HealthCare and the hospital or GPO that made the purchase. The small dealer, distributor, or OEM then manually enters the invoice into its own accounts receivable system.

5. *Payments are made via electronic funds transfer (EFT).*

Agfa HealthCare hasn't yet started using the EFT feature, says Vincent, although it soon may.

> Payments are not enforced yet, because the Medibuy exchange didn't offer this capability. Now, with GHX, we have the possibility of offering electronic funds transfers.

Vincent is also looking forward to adding other features provided by the Comergent platform, such as inventory management.

> The inventory management functionality hasn't yet been tested by us. The system consists of an XML–

> based architecture; therefore, the integration with other systems is done through sending and receiving real-time messages. The customer is picked first, based on volume and readiness, then the customer specifies the dealer/distributor of choice, then we connect the dealer/distributor to our hub and test the full transaction loop. In terms of messaging, the links are mainly ebXML or xCBL—they are the standards used in this industry.
>
> We are investigating all business processes in order to reduce, or eliminate, manual tasks. We continue deploying and utilizing the Comergent platform, and do not expect to add another software provider outside of SAP, which is our strategic backbone.

Contract management, price, and availability capabilities are also waiting in the wings, says Vincent.

> These functions are a prime objective of our implementation. They're already available from Comergent, but the exchange and our partners weren't ready to use it. Now, with GHX and bigger dealers/distributors connected to our hub, we will start testing those functionalities.

Plans for a lead generation capability are in the works, but have not yet solidified, says Vincent.

> The next step, which we are already investigating with Comergent, is lead generation. We want to enable lead management across different partners and different regions. The business case has been com-

pleted, and has been sent to our Belgium headquarters for approval. It has not been given top priority, however, since another corporate project, focusing on CRM technology, threatens to overlap the lead generation project.

The exchange environment gives Agfa HealthCare and its customers and partners a fine degree of control over their information, as well as the ability to view information from an array of perspectives, says Vincent.

The exchange provides a high degree of visibility to whatever is transacting across the marketplace from different views. The GPO, for example, has access to all GPO–related information; the buying side has access to everything it needs to buy; the selling side has access to everything it must sell; and the various manufacturers have access to whatever services and products they put online. So, you can have multiple partners, multiple roles, and everybody has real-time online access to the same type of information. As a result, we don't have reconciliation issues, and we don't have discrepancies between the different players.

Vincent began developing its Web services strategy in late 1999.

Agfa has a complex and lengthy approval process that slowed us down considerably. I presented the strategy in early 2000 to Agfa's board. We got the go-ahead in mid-2000. We then investigated the different available software packages and selected Comergent in late 2000. We started implementing the proof of concept in early 2001. After the proof of concept was accepted by our leadership, and understood by various management heads, we started deploying pilots. The system became operational in early 2003.

Although Vincent believes the exchange will eventually become her organization's primary business data conduit, the company still relies on a variety of older technologies.

We do not work only through the exchange. The majority of our current electronic volume is still transmitted through a conventional EDI VAN directly to our SAP system. We also have lots of manual entries; too many, really. We allow phone, fax, and e-mail orders that our customer services personnel has to process manually into our SAP system.

Vincent says Web services' modular foundation makes it easy to add new customers.

As long as the customer connects within the exchange's standard requirements, we can reuse the same map already tested with other customers. However, sometimes the customer doesn't want to be connected to the exchange; he wants to do business directly with us. Then, we have to handle the cross-mapping and routing of the information sent

> back and forth between its materials management system and our hub. The same thing is relative to the dealers; they can choose between a browser connectivity and a full integration. The browser doesn't generate any additional work, the full integration does, but we also need to work very closely with the dealer's IT team to make sure its ERP can receive and process our messages, and vice versa.

Prior to switching to Web services, Agfa HealthCare had very little control over the information it was sharing with customers and partners.

> It was a very unstructured and fragmented process. Everyone had different sets of data; everyone used incompatible formats and systems. Without Web services, none of these technologies were able to talk to each other.
>
> The value proposition we brought into play with Comergent and Web services was that this system allowed any technology, with any of five formats, to talk to each other. Therefore, we have a central hub between partners, customers, and manufacturers, allowing data sharing and collaboration. We have a flexible platform that can accept conventional EDI, flat file transfers, e-mail with attachments, SAP, IDOC, and, of course, XML. As a result, we don't require our partners or customers to modify their programs.
>
> I'm very convinced that we're bringing significant benefits to all of the parties involved. In order to

> really bank these benefits, however, you have to have critical mass. This process, unfortunately, is very slow. There's a lot of testing, mapping, training, and convincing that has to be accomplished. All of these factors slow down the implementation process. In health care, however, the goal is not to be revolutionary, or ahead of other industries.

Vincent says she's become a firm Web services supporter.

> I'm convinced about these standards: XML, SOAP, and all of the others. Since 1998, even before I moved to Agfa, I was already watching what was happening with Web services.
>
> When I proposed Web services to the board, they looked at me as if I was coming from Mars. Now, I think they understand the need, because most of our main partners are moving in the same direction. I think the adoption rate is improving.
>
> I have to admit, however, that it can be tough to convince high-level executives, particularly the leadership of big companies like Agfa, about the value of something like Web services. We're a 22,000-employee company, and the people that led this company in the past didn't always recognize the opportunities presented by electronic business, or any new technology. Because of the dot-com crash, they were very prudent and more than a little bit skeptical. Rather than make a massive upfront investment in something with a potentially limited immediate return, they wanted to implement new systems step-by-step.

Vincent notes that the Web services field, like many emerging technology markets, is flooded with vendors, offering a wide range of products. This can make it difficult for an organization to select the best products for specific Web services-related tasks.

> I think there are too many vendors. If you go to Google and search for Web services, you'll never finish reading about all the companies. One has to be careful to select companies that have been around for some time and that have products that deliver the benefits and the results customers want.

Still, Vincent has no regrets about selecting Comergent for Agfa HealthCare's Web services project.

> I would make the same choice, if I had to do it again; I would select Comergent right away. I think we picked the right vendor. But, if I were to repeat the selection process today, I would look at successful companies, see what types of packages they use, and then get references.

Despite some vendors' claims to the contrary, Vincent notes that Web services implementation isn't necessarily a snap.

> Going with Web services isn't as easy as buying a package that has open standards. Still, there are a lot of routines and subroutines that can ease the implementation and speed up the return on investment.

> But, most importantly, you have to fully understand your customers' expectations, your own issues, and know exactly the direction you want to move in to get the ROI you're looking for. All of this requires performing in-depth research and work.

Vincent feels that Web services give her better control over business processes.

> The direct benefit is the ownership of the relationship between our customers and partners. This allows us to anticipate customer expectations, paving the way toward both revenue and loyalty gains. If you have to rely on dealers, distributors, and OEMs just to understand what's happening between your own customers and the product and services you're indirectly selling, you're losing valuable time.

Web services also exposes Agfa HealthCare to potential customers.

> As soon as you display your electronic catalog to an exchange marketplace, this possibility exists. One can also use the technology to generate electronic leads and manage them better.
>
> For Vincent, the adoption of Web services is an ongoing process that requires continuous fine-tuning.
>
> The next step might be process engineering. We are setting team meetings to gather various functional leaders (owning part of the business processes to reengineering) to map the current processes, identify the disconnects, and propose alternatives to get

rid of any issue. We prioritize the business processes, based on our knowledge of current issues, to resolve outstanding issues, as soon as possible. Once we have the specification and benefits of the recommended alternative, we will decide on the technology enabler.

But we have to test first with customers and partners and identify what their next expectations are. For the time being, their expectations can be handled without changing too much internally, but I am convinced that, as soon as we move to the paperless, continuous flow of transaction information, they would change their process. That's to be expected.

So far, we have automated the current business processes and gain benefits through the elimination of manual activities; however, every new expectation and significant benefit we uncover requires changes. We need to simplify the way we do business today, and it will impact our internal processes and systems, too.

In the meantime, Vincent wishes that Web services technology was more adaptable.

I would like to have Web services more able to handle different formats, fields, and validations. Coping with these items requires a lot of technical expertise and is very costly.

Vincent also wishes that Web services offered better format translation tools.

> We have, for example, some unsophisticated partners that still use faxes. It would be nice to have a fax format recognition technology that would automatically convert fax documents into XML messages. This is something we currently have to do manually.

Vincent advises potential Web services adopters to start by building a solid e-business foundation.

> You have to start by clarifying your own e-business model, making sure that every aspect of its functionality will directly and positively impact your customers and partners. Having things look nice just isn't enough. Many Web sites, for example, will toss in all kinds of fancy functionality that, in fact, don't bring any value to either the customer or partner. Sticking with priorities, and having a better understanding of your customers' and partners' expectations, is where one should start.

She also advises potential adopters to carefully research Web services technologies before committing to specific products.

> You can't buy a package just because it has a good reputation and is backed by a large advertising budget. A large following alone doesn't mean that a product is good or right for your needs.

Finally, Vincent believes that Web services are ready for everyday use.

I've seen a lot of progress. Compared to where we started with our first implementation and where we are today, the speed, the functionality, and the quality of the data exchanges have all improved. Simply put, there are a lot of possibilities and a lot of opportunities for using Web services.

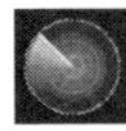

Chapter 10

Johnson Controls—Web Services in Control

Johnson Controls has expanded remarkably since Professor Warren Johnson founded the company in 1885 to manufacture his breakthrough invention: the electric room thermostat. Since its start, Milwaukee-based Johnson Controls has grown into a multibillion-dollar corporation, with worldwide leadership in two businesses: automotive systems and building controls.

Automakers outsource their interior system requirements to Johnson Controls to maximize quality and reduce costs. The company not only manufactures automotive interior systems; it designs, engineers, integrates, and delivers them globally. Likewise, the owners and managers of commercial, institutional, and government buildings worldwide turn to Johnson Controls to maximize comfort, productivity, safety, and energy efficiency. The company engineers, manufactures, and installs control systems that automate a building's heating, ventilating, and air conditioning, as well as its lighting and fire safety equipment.

It's in this latter area that the company is a pioneer adopter of Web services. Byron Hill is Johnson Control's director of systems and technology. He's using Web services to consolidate and streamline building management tasks.

> Our goal is to make the environment comfortable, provide for lighting, and so on. We essentially design systems and equipment that help manage a building's environment. We're also a part of the construction process and retrofit process in terms of how those projects get put together and how they're managed, even when it's not our content. We also know the problems that the construction industry and owners have in designing and integrating building systems. We're an integrator, and that's where Web services play an important role for us.
>
> We've always told our customers, "We'll take care of you, and we'll make sure that everything works." But getting different systems to talk to each other can be a painful process and very expensive. Fortunately, we have experience in this field because we do it over and over again at multiple sites. We have more than 300 branches worldwide. Integrating with other systems is our business.
>
> Sometimes, integration is as simple as connecting to a piece of equipment—a motor, or something like that. But often it's something very complicated, as in talking with an entire building management system. Web services can make those integrations much easier to do. It gives us much richer content, particularly if I'm not even sure what system I'm going to

> run into out there, what system I'm going to have to integrate with.

Web services are helping Johnson Controls adapt to a rapidly changing, information-oriented world. Historically, components of building automation systems have relied on proprietary operating systems, communicating with each other using proprietary protocols. Although industry-specific standards for device communication (like the BACNET protocol) have recently emerged, many IT departments view these protocols and the devices that use them as proprietary.

> Building systems traditionally have had their own networking infrastructure, separate from IT. Now, these two types of networks are beginning to blend. While in the IT world, there are usually very stringent standards covering just about everything, we didn't have these types of requirements within the building world. But now, for us to be able to communicate and use an external company's infrastructure, we have to adhere to certain standards.
>
> Web services present a new standard for connecting systems and the basic exchange of information. It's something we can take advantage of, rather than have the building industry try to figure out another way that's going to be friendly to IT in terms of usability and trust. So, we really see Web services as a strategy to help us in integrating systems.

Johnson Controls has developed the first Web services–based facility management platform. The Metasys building management system uses Web services to provide operational efficiencies and cost savings to owners of nonresidential buildings. The technology allows businesses and other organizations to easily interconnect and manage a wide range of facility systems.

In the past, corporations, schools, hospitals, and government organizations were limited in how they could operate and optimize their facilities. Power, heating, air conditioning, lighting, fire, and security systems came in proprietary packages, which restricted how and from where they could be controlled. It also limited how data from those systems could be accessed and transformed into meaningful information.

Johnson Controls's technology not only integrates and simplifies the operation of building systems, but, for the first time, links them to management information systems. This allows enterprise-wide connectivity, monitoring, data acquisition, and reporting of vital operational information. As a result, businesses and other organizations can establish healthier, more productive, and safer environments at less cost and effort. Previously, such integration, when possible, could only be achieved with hours of computer programming to create customized connections for every individual application.

> We have instances where we essentially run the facility for the customer. We own that part of the budget, we own the people that are in the facility management part of the business. We know the pain of having to take someone else's box and trying to make it work and get those things done. That's how we're a little different than most of our competitors.

Hill offers the example of how Johnson Controls serves a school that, in order to save money, has an automated system that coordinates environmental services with class schedules.

> Say a college or university is putting together class schedules. Right now, once they do the schedules, they program them into the building management system. Now, with Web services, we have the ability to share the schedule between the two systems. I can actually use their scheduler and consume that as a Web service, bringing it into my system and automatically programming how the lights come on, when the heating comes on, and so forth. It's all based on the classroom schedule.

For Johnson Controls and its clients, Web services provide benefits in three key areas:

1. *Reduced Expenses.* The Metasys system eliminates the need for proprietary workstations and software, which can result in significant savings on installation costs. For example, giving multiple users access to the system can be provided at much less than it would cost to provide the same access to a conventional building automation system.
2. *Distributed Access.* The Web services–based Metasys system provides access to real-time information anytime, anywhere through desktops, laptops, Personal Digital Assistants (PDAs), or home PCs. This operational flexibility can improve employee productivity and reduce an enterprise's operating costs.

3. *Meaningful Data.* The Metasys system transforms data into useful information that is easily accessible to any interested manager, not just facilities staff. For example, in a critical care environment, a clinical manager can use the Metasys system to access a real-time, single-screen snapshot of the status of isolation rooms—including a patient's name, diagnosis, when he was admitted to the room, who occupied that room previously and that person's diagnosis, and the room's temperature, humidity, and status of the isolation air-handling system. Previously, such information only was available by logging into different systems, from different workstations.

These benefits are possible because standard Web services technology is built into the core of the Metasys system. Web services allow two or more computer applications—say a conference room scheduling system, employee database, and building security system—to share information and work cooperatively over the Internet. Web services are the tools that finally enable the connectivity between enterprises and applications envisioned when the Internet became widely accessible in the early 1990s.

The types of buildings Johnson Controls manages through Web services include just about every type of commercial structure imaginable.

> We have over a billion square feet of office space under our control, either by our products or our services. That covers all markets—health care, education from K-12 through higher education. There are also what we call "critical facilities," such as financial

> institutions and data centers, drug companies, and high-tech manufacturing. Then there's commercial real estate, too—the office buildings. They all need building management systems.

In an increasingly mobile world, building facility personnel aren't always seated at a dedicated workstation. People now need to access and act on information in building automation systems from any location, and through the broadest possible range of devices. Johnson Controls's Metasys technology is designed to meet this need.

> To make the information in our systems more valuable, we need to make it more accessible. Customers want facilities solutions that are based on Internet technology—systems that they can access with Web browsers, smart client applications, and mobile devices.

Many of Johnson Controls's customers have very specific needs.

> Consider how we work with an airport. When a flight is coming in, the flight information system sends the information to our system to turn on the lights, air, electricity, and other services at the appropriate terminal gate. Then, once the people get in and the plane has been docked for a certain period, the system will turn everything off and send that information back to the flight information system. The building management system will also perform the billing for that terminal.

Web services also allow Johnson Controls to translate control data into end user–accessible information.

> You've probably seen in some of the newer hotels flight information that feeds directly to a display. We never expected that someday we would be talking to a flight management system, but it's a practical application we need. That's because we have to know flight schedules, so we can turn on the environmental controls inside the terminal. Now we can also make that information available to hotels and their customers.

Johnson Controls has built its Web services initiative with the Microsoft .NET platform. The company also uses the Microsoft Windows XP Embedded operating system for its supervisory controller, relying on Web services to expose the controller's functionality. The hardware is a National Geode GX1 CPU, running at 300MHz with 256MB of RAM and 256MB of flash memory.

> About three years ago, we were looking at rearchitecting our building management system, where information was the key driver in being able to talk to and integrate with other applications in the enterprise. A customer would ask us, for example, to integrate into their PeopleSoft system.
>
> We looked at a number of different protocols and wanted something that was very IT–friendly. At the time, there were really only three companies that really presented a set of tools that allowed us to develop Web services: Sun, IBM, and Microsoft. At least

> these were the ones that were fairly mature. We picked Microsoft, because they had an operating system that we used in some of our equipment.
>
> We're using the .NET framework to manage our code. But we also have some things that are not managed by .NET, which are mostly on the COM portion of our architecture. That's because we have things that are outside of Web services that we need in the building world.

Before deploying Web services, Hill relied on an assortment of integration technologies. He says the arrival of Web services has made his life easier and his shop more productive.

> If you think about the things that came before Web services—Dynamic Data Exchange, DLLs, and all kinds of APIs—they all required special programming. If the programmer went away, and you needed to change the code, you had to redevelop everything. So, we needed a more standard way of interacting with other applications, or other systems. Even within our own organization, as we integrate our platforms, we're doing it through a set of Web services. We're not going to add a lot of special protocols, because it would take us a lot longer to get those two systems to talk to each other.
>
> The beauty of Web services is that you can have published Web services, the ones you tell everyone about, and unpublished ones you wouldn't tell anyone about. That would include, for example, the way building automation and security systems talk to each other.

Web services make it easier to guide developers working in specific areas, says Hill.

> The beauty is, I can essentially tell the developers doing security, "This is the way you talk to the building management system," and they can write to that. And it works the first time out.

Hill notes that Web services also speeds development time by allowing Johnson Controls to easily work with outside developers.

> The technology allows us to shop out applications that we probably couldn't get done from a resource standpoint, or a timing standpoint. It makes it a lot easier for us to give the task to a third party and say, "Hey, here's my blueprint for talking to my system—develop this application." Web services present a rich set of tools, and a lot of external parties can develop applications much faster than in the past.

Hill notes that the Web services vendors are targeting the market with different approaches.

> I think the vendors are kind of running neck and neck. To me, the race is to get a wide range of developers to use your tool set. That's what Microsoft is selling. Microsoft is looking at the developers as their customers. IBM, on the other hand, really wants to control the back office. So both companies have different objectives, but I think the race right now is between those two companies.

For Hill, one of the key advantages to using Web services is the ability to easily adapt existing software so it can interact with external applications.

> We don't have to redevelop everything. We're able to put a wrapper around our own middleware, allowing us to essentially translate data into a standard format. So Web services allow us to communicate with outside applications, an ability we didn't have before.

Hill says organizations have to be realistic about Web services' ability to solve real-world business problems.

> It's important to be very practical about why you're using Web services. There's a lot of hype in the media surrounding Web services. You'll see the idea, for example, of having a universal directory that's going to be out there and will know where all the Web services pieces are. But that's probably going to be a second- or third-generation technology. Right now, the Web services capability that offers the most value is integration with known systems. In this area, Web services provide a level of interoperability that didn't exist before. So, rather than getting caught up in the hype, you'll have something of practical value.

Like many Web services users, Hill feels that UDDI needs more work before it's ready for real-world use.

> UDDI will mature as the industry matures. You'll have groups that will develop UDDIs for a particular industry. But until the Web services field matures, they're not going to be there.

The only other major concern I have is Web services security. You can never say enough about that. It's something that's still in the works, but it will mature. We've taken steps to address security in Metasys, but it also needs to be addressed for general Web services. Right now, not all Web services are exposed, but security really becomes an issue when you start exposing Web services externally. If you're using Web services within your own back-office infrastructure, however, it's not as big an issue.

Before adopting Web services, it's important to carefully study how the technology can improve a particular process, says Hill.

You need to measure the benefit. Ask yourself, "Am I able to do things faster, or am I going to be able to get richer information?" You have to design your metrics around those considerations. That's what we did. We went through that exercise, and it took a little bit of time, but we did it for the right reasons.

Hill believes that Web services are ready for everyday use.

Yes, I think they're ready for prime time. I think the tool sets are now mature enough. We've actually added on quite a few staff members in our engineering group, and we're able to get people up to speed fairly quickly with the tool set. You rarely find a lot of people with Web services experience, so we're sort of training them as we go. There are a lot worse things than Web services in the IT world that don't

> have as much industry backing, or companies really pushing for its success.

Hill says the proof of Web services' value lies in its growing acceptance among enterprises of all types and sizes.

> Forget the hype, you can tell that Web services are useful from the adoption rate, particularly within the IT organizations. IT is all over Web services, because they really address some of their pain.
>
> You think about the customer. You think about how Web services will reduce some of their pain, or take away some of the pain I have in the things I'm working on. When it comes to integrating systems together, Web services addresses these needs directly.

Hill doesn't feel that his decision to adopt Web services was particularly risky.

> While we're an early adopter, we don't feel like we're way out on a limb. That's because Web services addresses something we were already doing—now we're just using a different mechanism to do it. We think we've found a much better way of working with our customers—much easier, much more efficient—and it's a standard that's acceptable to others. That was a big benefit for us.
>
> So we adopted Web services for very practical reasons—it's an added benefit that others are also adopting it. We probably would have gone to Web

> services anyway, because they're core to what we do. On the other hand, we're glad we found something that was readily acceptable by others.

The fundamental reason for adopting Web services, however, was financial.

> We have to make money at it, so that quickly narrows your choices.

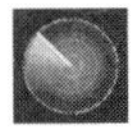

Chapter 11

The Stencil Group—Reflections and Predictions on Web Services

Located in San Francisco, The Stencil Group is a focused consulting and analysis firm that works with enterprise software companies to understand their customers' business objectives and IT priorities. The firm's services support product strategy and product marketing needs.

The Stencil Group's current research emphasis on Web services reflects the firm's view that the shift toward service-based computing represents a new, distinct stage in the ongoing evolution of the enterprise software market. IT organizations are realizing significant strategic benefit from this shift, but the impact on software vendors is more complex.

Brent Sleeper is a cofounder and partner in The Stencil Group, and he leads the Stencil Group's Web services research and consulting practice. As a leading independent expert on Web services, Sleeper is the author of many articles and frequently speaks at industry events. Before cofounding The Stencil Group, Brent served in senior roles with e-business consulting firms iXL and NetResponse. Brent also worked with National Public Radio and the State of Texas. He's a graduate of Carleton College.

Sleeper believes that today's Web services field is the result of a gradual technological development process stretching back over the past decade.

> I think you can point to specific events, namely the development of SOAP and the development of XML before that. One can even trace the origin of Web services back to the Common Object Request Broker Architecture (CORBA). In other words, there has been an entire ongoing series of technical developments and architectural best practices that have come together in the last couple of years. So it's hard to say exactly when Web services started, because it's part of a revolution that's been going on for ten years or more. On the other hand, you can say that all of these solutions started to reach a critical mass in the last couple of years.

Compared to Web services, CORBA was a difficult, hard-to-use, and ultimately unpopular technology, says Sleeper.

> In a lot of ways, CORBA tried to do what Web services are now trying to do. But it was seriously flawed. For one thing, it was very, very complex. Therefore, it only had a few, hard-core organizations that embraced it and started deploying it. Everybody else felt it was too much work and not worth the trouble.

Web services mark a significant improvement over CORBA, says Sleeper.

> Compared to CORBA, Web services are solving similar problems—it's all about how you connect multiple systems. In other words, how do you design software in such a way that various elements, or components, execute on different computers and in different organizations over a network? The guiding principle behind most Web services design is to achieve integration in the simplest way possible. Vendors and adopters are both shooting for: "Let's get a couple things right," rather than "Let's try to solve every single problem."

Sleeper believes that Web services represent an opportunity for enterprises to derive greater IT benefits and efficiencies.

> Over the past eighteen months, my organization has talked to about 125 IT organizations that are either adopting Web services, or working toward adopting them in one way or the other. What these organizations are telling us is that they have some fundamental IT issues that they believe Web services will help them address.
>
> Perhaps the most direct benefit they expect to receive from Web services is the integration of different systems. From a strictly technical perspective, there are lots of benefits available along the lines of interoperability, particularly the reuse of existing systems. In light of the fact that there are products from various IT vendors that run on different platforms,

> we've come to the conclusion that the only way to deal with these differences is to accept them, instead of trying to pigeonhole all of our IT into just one approach. A single platform isn't always viable; sometimes it's just not realistic.
>
> So how do we deal with the fact that we must live with multiple systems? Well, it's by tying the systems together and connecting them in a way that doesn't cost hundreds of thousands, or even multiple millions, of dollars. Those are the amounts that enterprises have traditionally paid for integration products. The challenge is integration and interoperability—doing it in a way that is cost-effective.

Sleeper feels that Web services have just started entering the IT mainstream.

> If you look at classic adoption models, we're certainly on the cusp of moving beyond early adopters and entering the mainstream. But Web services are still in their early stages.
>
> One thing that's interesting about this particular wave of IT is that many of the early adopters aren't your classic technologist types of organizations—companies that are always trying out the latest and greatest. Technologist firms are definitely working with Web services. But one of the things that we were a little bit surprised to recognize is that there's another group of organizations that isn't necessarily driven by the technical issues that typically drive early adopters. We're seeing a much more bottom-line business focus among these organizations.

> They're approaching Web services with the idea: "How does this help me change the way I pay for IT?" "How does this make my IT more cost-effective?" "How does this allow me to tackle projects, or initiatives, that I may not otherwise be able to do cost-effectively?" As a result, these organizations aren't really approaching Web services from the classic technologist or IT architecture perspective.

Sleeper sees IBM and Microsoft as two current Web services leaders. But he notes that many smaller companies are also playing a big hand in the technology's development.

> A couple companies—IBM and Microsoft—are on the vanguard of Web services. They're the firms that are really pushing the technology. From a marketing perspective and from a standards-proposal perspective, these firms are certainly very aggressive in their practices.
>
> But there's also another aspect to the situation that's recognizable, if you look at current IT trends; there's a much broader Web services movement than the efforts of just these two companies. There are other companies, big and small, even independent developers, that are also promoting Web services as a practical solution. These vendors have been, frankly, the key to some of the early technology developments. For example, SOAP is often credited to Microsoft, which certainly played a role in its development. However, there were also some much smaller companies that were in there working on the SOAP proposal as well.

Powering the rapid growth of Web services is support from both software developers and IT managers, says Sleeper.

> Web services' popularity has a sort of grassroots element to it. So many of the early projects that we looked at were really taken up at a developer's own initiative. He had a problem to solve, typically an integration problem, and the individual said, "Hey, SOAP helps me solve this particular problem really well, and it's easy to use!" That kind of grassroots support, bubbling up from down below, laid the foundation for some of the more strategic, top-down stuff we're seeing today.

Sleeper compares today's Web services steamroller to the evolution of another groundbreaking technology.

> I compare it to the World Wide Web and the Internet as we know it today. That technology, too, was rolled out in organizations. There was, typically, an independent, innovative, grassroots kind of IT person who said, "Hey, I can put up a Web site, and look how it allows me to share information." That attitude started to snowball. As a result, within a couple of years, having a cohesive Internet strategy became a major IT issue. I think we're seeing that same evolution in Web services today.

Sleeper believes that the benefits of Web services are accessible to just about any enterprise, regardless of its size or focus.

> If you look at the minimum requirements for a developer to use Web services, it's open to just about anybody. That's a big part of its appeal, the fact that you don't have to make an up-front investment of multiple millions of dollars in order to make it work.

Yet it's large enterprises that have driven much of the early Web services growth, says Sleeper.

> Some of the early case studies show that Web services tend to be driven by large organizations—sort of a classic, Fortune 500–type of company that's trying to figure out ways of making their IT work more cost-effectively with smaller partners. If you look at how EDI rolled out, it was typically only the biggest companies that paid for the technology. As a result, you might have companies like Boeing and Lockheed joining together via EDI.

More than twenty years ago, EDI emerged as a format for the electronic communication of business transactions, such as purchase orders, invoices, bills of lading, shipping schedules, and payments between organizations. The technology worked well in an e-business world that was dominated by big corporations that relied on value-added networks (VANs) and other point-to-point trading technologies. Yet, a growing number of organizations are gradually realizing that the old warhorse may not be up to the demands of twenty-first century B2B transactions. Ganging up against EDI are the technology's high cost (estimated by analysts at anywhere between one dollar and twenty dollars per transaction), as well as the need for users to maintain extensive programming resources and an elaborate support infrastructure. Lower-cost Web services, however, allow a large enterprise to link to much smaller business partners.

> One of the things we're seeing in some of the early-use cases is a company like Boeing not only reaching out to its first-tier suppliers, but also to its second- and third-tier suppliers. You start to get into some of those almost "mom-and-pop" types of manufacturing companies that are further down in the food chain. Now even these small organizations can afford to tie in and use the Web browser as an extranet-type system. They can take that approach and extend it into an automated system. I think that's a really promising development.

Leading-edge Web services development, however, still remains mostly concentrated in the hands of large enterprises, says Sleeper.

> Certainly the more complex, more strategic Web services initiatives are being lead by classic, big IT organizations. But they're not the only ones able to use Web services; I think that's what's different this time around.

Although Web services allow enterprises to explore new business opportunities, most early adopters are using the technology to solve existing problems in a cost-effective manner.

> For internal integration, a real common use right now is creating interfaces to big, old, legacy mainframe

> systems that have been around for years, and probably aren't going away. Organizations can use Web services to tie those systems into more modern and, very often, Web-based systems. That's definitely a common trend we're seeing—taking legacy apps and inserting them into the IT mainstream.

Although most early Web services implementations focused on internal integration, adopters are increasingly looking to the technology to serve their external integration needs, says Sleeper.

Today, it's not always internal. Most deployments still are internal—on order of about two-thirds of them. But another third deal with partner-to-partner integration, and that's a significant development.

> A common external Web services application is partner-to-partner integration. In particular, we're seeing big company-to-small company integration, and it's being done in a cost-effective way. We're also seeing more organizations using Web services to deal with portals. They're taking all of their automated systems and tying them into a user interface—a dashboard.

Sleeper points to myCIGNA.com, which uses portal technology to provide self-service functions, as an example of how Web services are making life easier for both enterprises and end users.

> That's a classic example of how enterprises are using this technology. It's something that would have been very difficult to create before the arrival of Web services. Sure, they could have done it—but

> only at an enormous cost. That's what's different with Web services—you can do a whole range of applications that may not have been cost-effective with earlier technologies.
>
> In the past, something like myCIGNA.com would have required a lot of custom development work. You could get it done, but it would cost a lot of money. Plus, there was a slew of technical problems associated with earlier portal development technologies. For most organizations, it simply wasn't worth the effort. The return was marginal, and most companies just weren't going to do it.
>
> Web services lower the financial bar for these kinds of projects. The technology might end up saving a company $50,000 in development costs over the long term. That's not a huge amount of money in the eyes of many businesses, but if you can do this sort of development work cost-effectively, the savings add up. With Web services, you can increase the reach and decrease the amount of investment you need up front. This opens the way to an entire new terrain of automation and, in economic terms, a potentially large boost in productivity gains.

Although Sleeper feels that Web services are definitely ready for widespread use, he notes that some technical work remains to be done. He identifies the two most pressing needs:

> If you look at surveys of IT executives, certainly on the top of those lists are two prime concerns: "I want to figure out how to deal with security in a systematic

> way," and "I want to figure out how to deal with a complex, transaction-based system."

Yet Sleeper is optimistic that enhancements to Web services will eventually become available.

> The executives I've talked to feel that it's not a question of how today's Web services problems will be solved. It's more like, "When will they be solved?" They're pretty confident the answers will happen.

Despite continuing improvements to Web services standards and software, system design remains a big concern for most adopters, says Sleeper.

> Many of the issues executives are currently struggling with relates to specific design processes. In other words, how can an organization design new distributive systems in a way that really meets business needs? Organizations want to know how not to get stuck in the same trap, like they did with CORBA. With COBRA, everything was so fine-grained that it became very technical, and very difficult to create useful business processes.
>
> Executives want to know, "How do I design my Web services applications at the appropriate level of granularity?" That's a term executives often use. They want to match a Web service to a specific step in the business process and get the right degree of correlation. This is, frankly, the toughest issue adopters are dealing with from a technology and design perspective.

Adopters are also struggling with cost and management concerns. Sleeper notes that executives launching an entirely new software development approach usually view the task as a difficult and perilous undertaking.

> They're asking, "OK, who can pay for this?" "Who's going to have the bottom-line accountability for making sure the system works?" These are issues that are broader than just Web services, but Web services have a real impact in these areas.

Sleeper believes that, in addition to interoperability, Web services' primary benefits are in the areas of enhanced cost-effectiveness and operational flexibility.

> Cost-effectiveness allows IT organizations to automate processes and create applications that may not have been financially feasible before the availability of Web services. As far as flexibility goes, one of the things we're hearing again and again is that enterprises want to be as flexible as possible. They don't want IT to determine what they can do, or can't do, with their business; they want it to be the other way around. They want IT to build and support whatever business opportunity exists. That's one of the real drivers, as well as the philosophical buy-in, to the Web services model—the idea that an organization can distribute systems across business processes. With Web services, we have modular solutions that we can put together and break up, if we need to. So flexibility is important and, from a business perspective, it's been a major benefit.

Sleeper believes that Web services will evolve rapidly over the next few years, changing to meet new business needs and preferences.

> There will certainly be an ongoing, evolving stack of technology. If you look at how a lot of the early Web services standards were designed, they're clearly intended to be layered on top of one another. We're going to continue to layer new functions, new products, and new standards on top of that base, and it will always continue—it's probably never going to stop. As new areas are explored, there will always be a new problem and someone will try to figure out how to solve it.

The Web services areas that will change first are the technologies that currently fail to meet enterprises' most pressing needs.

> Better security and support for complex transactions are two key areas. These issues need to be addressed via standards and via software products.
>
> There's also an entire range of strategic, very expensive, mission-critical business processes that could benefit from Web services. But I wouldn't yet throw these vital processes at Web services—the technology just isn't there. However, I do believe that solutions will trickle in over the next couple of years. In the meantime, if I'm an enterprise manager, I can start with my simple, less critical processes and obtain some learning and experience.

Sleeper's advice to organizations considering the use of Web services is to advance incrementally.

Don't try to do it all at once. Take a small step, but do get started. There's relatively little risk, and there's a lot to be gained and a lot to learn. But definitely get started.

Also, embrace the idea that you will have multiple software providers helping you. You certainly can buy into one particular vendor's approach, but the real benefit, from an IT perspective, is the concept of interoperability. It's the idea of not getting locked into a single vendor's approach. So, hedge your bets. Force your vendors to get along. Don't let them force you to walk their line.

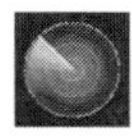

Appendix

Products and Services

Here's a closer look at the Web services–related products and services used by the enterprises profiled in the preceding chapters.

Chapter One—CIGNA

IBM WebSphere Application Server

IBM WebSphere Application Server is a high-performance and scalable transaction engine for dynamic e-business applications. The server is designed to provide a foundation for supporting on-demand business applications.

IBM
New Orchard Road
Armonk, NY 10504
800-426-4968
www.ibm.com

Netegrity SiteMinder

Netegrity SiteMinder provides enterprises with a security infrastructure for managing user access to complex e-business sites. SiteMinder supports real-time transactions and Web services. SiteMinder is a software platform of shared services that includes single sign-on, authentication management (who you are), and entitlement management (what you are allowed to do on the site).

Netegrity
52 Second Avenue
Waltham, MA 02451
800-325-9870
www.netegrity.com

Sun ONE Directory Server (formerly Sun iPlanet Directory Server)

The Sun ONE Directory Server provides a central repository for storing and managing identity profiles, access privileges, applications, and network resource information. The integrated, LDAP–based server helps improve security, ensuring that appropriate access control policies are enforced across all communities, applications, and services on a global basis.

Sun Microsystems
4150 Network Circle
Santa Clara, CA 95054
800-555-9786
www.sun.com

Yahoo! PortalBuilder

Yahoo! PortalBuilder is designed to provide the foundation for a complete portal solution. The product provides a scalable technology platform on which enterprises can build, manage, and run B2E, B2B, and B2C portals. Yahoo! PortalBuilder is designed to provide a simple, function-rich experience right out of the box. It aims to deliver on all the key portal software requirements: content aggregation, application integration, rich personalization, and flexible presentation. Open, Java-based, and fully J2EE–compliant, Yahoo! PortalBuilder is also highly extensible, virtually platform-agnostic, and vendor-neutral. Because it's fast and easy for administrators to set up and maintain, a Yahoo!-powered portal can be implemented within a few weeks, rather than a few months.

Yahoo!
701 First Avenue
Sunnyvale, CA 94089
408-349-3300
www.yahoo.com

Chapter Two—Putnam Lovell NBF Securities

Appshop

Appshop features custom-hosted software that provides financial linking and integration services.

Appshop
48089 Fremont Boulevard

Fremont, CA 94538
510-353-2900
www.appshop.com

Salesforce.com Enterprise Edition

Salesforce.com Enterprise Edition is designed to help organizations maximize their operating capabilities by eliminating the burdens of software ownership. Turning the conventional model of software ownership on its head, Enterprise Edition allows users to simplify and standardize complex customer operations through a single, online solution that can be rapidly deployed across multiple departments and divisions. Salesforce .com Enterprise Edition doesn't require users to purchase or install a single line of code.

Salesforce.com
The Landmark @ One Market
Suite 300
San Francisco, CA 94105
415-901-7000
www.salesforce.com

BlueMatrix Research

BlueMatrix Research is designed to provide a complete technical infrastructure for enterprise research efforts. Authoring, work flow, editorial, compliance, document warehousing, document repurposing, and "one-click," multichannel document distribution are all handled by this integrated software. Built for the Web, BlueMatrix handles, from front to back, the preparation, review, compliance, release, and distribution of all equity research output. The browser-based environment can be customized to meet specific look and function specifications.

BlueMatrix
12 East 20th Street
3rd Floor
New York, NY 10003
212-475-9330
www.bluematrix.com

Grand Central Communications Enterprise Solution

Grand Central Communications Enterprise Solution orchestrates automated business processes through a network service. The software provides an environment in which customers automatically receive reports without the need for manual intervention.

Grand Central Communications
50 Fremont Street
San Francisco, CA 94105
415-344-3200
www.grandcentral.com

Chapter Three—Hewlett-Packard

Microsoft .NET Framework

Microsoft .NET is software that connects people, information, systems, and devices through the use of Web services. Web services are a combination of protocols that enable computers to work together by exchanging messages. Web services are based on the standard protocols of XML, SOAP, and WSDL, which allow them to interoperate across platforms and programming languages.

Microsoft Visual Studio. NET

Visual Studio .NET is a tool for building Microsoft .NET-connected applications for Microsoft Windows and the Web. The software aims to dramatically increase developer productivity, enabling new business and enterprise opportunities. The product provides tools for designing, building, testing, and deploying Web services and applications, as well as sharing best practices and guidelines in a team environment.

Microsoft
1 Microsoft Way
Redmond, WA 98052-6399
425-882-8080
www.microsoft.com

Borland JBuilder

Borland JBuilder is a cross-platform environment for building enterprise Java applications. The software is designed to simplify Web and EJB development with two-way visual designers and rapid deployment to leading J2EE platform application servers. Developers can enhance their productivity with UML code visualization, refactoring, code formatting, HotSwap debugging, unit testing, and version control integration.

Together Control Center

Together Control Center aims to accelerate development for enterprises using Java and Java 2 Enterprise Edition (J2EE) application servers, allowing them to build comprehensive e-business and enterprise applications. Together Control Center also supports teams using C++, IDL, and XML, delivering wider coverage and support for large development organizations.

Borland Software
100 Enterprise Way
Scotts Valley, CA 95066
831-431-1000
www.borland.com

BEA WebLogic Application Server

The BEA WebLogic Application Server is a standards-based product that's designed to handle the crucial tasks associated with application development and deployment. The server's capabilities range from integrating enterprise systems and databases to delivering Web services and collaboration over the Internet.

BEA Systems
2315 N. 1st Street
San Jose, CA 95131
800-817-4232
www.beasys.com

Eclipse

Eclipse is an open-source, integrated development environment for tool integration. More details are available at www.eclipse.org.

Jboss

JBoss is an open-source application server. More details are available at www.jboss.org.

Chapter Four—Vail Resorts

Datalex BookIt! Suite

The Datalex BookIt! Suite is a family of products that enables airlines, travel portals, travel suppliers, and distributors to market a broad spectrum of travel products to consumers, corporations, and travel agencies. The suite is a combination of solution-specific Internet booking engines, a fares database, and a choice of external interfaces that support multiple Web access technologies, including browsers, mobile phones, personal digital assistants (PDAs), and digital television. BookIt! Suite integrates air, car, hotel, tour, cruise, and vacation package data from multiple sources and presents it in a user-friendly format on a variety of Web-access platforms for inquiry and booking operations.

BookIt! Fares

BookIt! Fares is a fares booking and management system that provides a comprehensive choice of valid negotiated fare and availability options for all types of air itineraries, including complex multisector itineraries.

The complex pricing logic employed by the system validates all net fare quotations for higher intermediate fares, open jaws, double-open jaws, and complex stopover routings, offering instant, accurate, and available fare quotations via GUI or Web browser interface. Fare classes and/or carriers can also be mixed on multisector routes.

Datalex
Howth House, Harbour Road
Dublin, Ireland
+353-1-839-1787
www.datalex.com

BEA WebLogic Application Server

(See Chapter Three.)

Chapter Five—Fairfax County, Virginia

Microsoft .NET Framework

(See Chapter Three.)

Microsoft Visual Studio .NET

(See Chapter Three.)

Microsoft ASP .NET

Microsoft ASP .NET is a programming framework that's built on a common language runtime. The technology is used on a server to build powerful Web applications.

Microsoft Windows Server (formerly .Net Server)

Microsoft Windows Server is a multipurpose operating system that's capable of handling a diverse set of server roles, including Web services.

Microsoft
1 Microsoft Way
Redmond, WA 98052-6399
425-882-8080
www.microsoft.com

The webMethods Integration Platform

The webMethods Integration Platform is a solution for managing business processes that link enterprise software packages, legacy systems, databases, work flows, and Web services, both within and across enterprises. The webMethods software offers a standards-based, massively scalable integration platform that's equipped to help organizations build and manage enterprise-class integration networks.

webMethods
3930 Pender Drive
Fairfax, VA 22030
703-460-2500
www.webmethods.com

Chapter Six—Dow Jones & Company

BizTalk

The BizTalk Server allows the deployment and management of Web services. The product enables users to build and deploy integrated business processes within their enterprise and with partners. Through the freely downloadable BizTalk Adaptor for Web Services, developers can create Web services that provide synchronous access to BizTalk Server applications without writing code.

Microsoft
1 Microsoft Way
Redmond, WA 98052-6399
425-882-8080
www.microsoft.com

Chapter Seven—Regular Baptist Press

ColdFusion

ColdFusion is designed to help enterprises build and deploy powerful Web applications and Web services with less training time and fewer lines of code than ASP, PHP, and JSP. Available in versions that support industry-leading J2EE application servers, ColdFusion enables Web application developers to harness the power of the Java platform.

Macromedia
600 Townsend Street
San Francisco, CA 94103
415-252-2000
www.macromedia.com

Chapter Eight—Eric Scott Custom Products

Made2Manage Enterprise Resource Planning

The Made2Manage Enterprise Resource Planning (M2M ERP) back-office platform captures enterprise data in a centralized system. By integrating all production processes into a single database, M2M ERP can handle all facets of an enterprise's operations

Made2Manage VIP

Made2Manage VIP offers Web-based functionality on a subscriber basis. The platform provides customer-facing, Web-enabled applications that provide customers with self-service access to key business processes and information. The solution relies primarily on the Microsoft SQL Server, SOAP, and XML.

Made2Manage Link

Made2Manage Link enterprise integration services automate communications between an enterprise business system and other business systems or trading exchanges.

Made2Manage Systems
3 Parkwood Crossing
50 E. 96th Street, Suite 300
Indianapolis, IN 46240
317-249-1200
www.made2manage.com

Chapter Nine—Agfa HealthCare

Comergent C3 Advisor

Comergent C3 Advisor is designed to give customers an optimal buying experience by guiding them through the entire product selection and comparison process. The C3 Advisor aims to minimize the time it takes customers to find products that meet their specific requirements, while providing sellers with customer data for post-sale analysis. The application customizes selling scenarios according to customers' experience levels, buying habits, and/or contractual relationships with the seller. The product's goal is to ensure that customers get exactly what they need, while reducing the number of calls to the seller's customer service representatives.

Comergent C3 Analyzer

Comergent C3 Analyzer is designed to give enterprises insight into their demand chain. The C3 Analyzer generates comprehensive analytics that can be used to help an organization effectively market, sell, and service an entire channel, ultimately increasing revenue and reducing costs. The C3 Analyzer provides insight into the commerce activities across all sales channels. Reports generated by the software enable organizations to anticipate market opportunities, improve forecasting, and understand channel business and customer-buying preferences.

Comergent C3 Profile Manager

Comergent C3 Profile Manager is a comprehensive information repository that stores demographic, business, and transaction data on customers and channel partners. The information is then leveraged by other Comergent applications to give customers and partners personalized information and application views on products, pricing, promotions, and other areas. The system is designed to be scalable to accommodate rapid data growth and flexible enough to respond to an enterprise's multiple needs and hierarchies. The C3 Profile Manager also provides an intuitive administrative user interface that allows even nontechnical business users to easily maintain the system.

Comergent C3 Product Manager

Comergent C3 Product Manager lets enterprises aggregate product data from internal and external sources and structure a coherent set of product information within an e-business platform. The C3 Product Manager provides central management of all e-business aspects, including product data syndication and import, product bundling, product lifetime, and product succession management.

Comergent C3 MarketLink

Comergent C3 MarketLink gives suppliers control over the sales process, including the ability to highlight products and/or services and avoid commoditization. The software allows enterprises to gain valuable insights into their customers' buying behavior by bringing them to their site. Organizations can ensure customer satisfaction and avoid expensive order rework by providing customers with the most up-to-date product information.

Comergent C3 Partner.com

Comergent C3 Partner.com is designed to help enterprises deliver complete solutions to customers by integrating complementary products, fulfillment offerings, and partner services. With C3 Partner.com, an enterprise and its partners can jointly sell and market to customers, respond to quote requests, accept orders, and provide fulfillment updates. The C3 Partner.com platform instantly enables an organization's selling partners, requiring only a Web browser. The software's nonintrusive method of partner enablement is designed to bolster the quick adoption of collaborative commerce initiatives, regardless of the selling partners' level of technical sophistication.

Comergent Technologies
1201 Radio Road
Redwood City, CA 94065
650-232-6000
www.comergent.com

Chapter Ten—Johnson Controls

Microsoft .NET Framework

(See Chapter Three.)

Microsoft Visual Studio .NET

(See Chapter Three.)

The Microsoft Windows XP Embedded Operating System

Windows XP Embedded is a version of the company's XP operating system that's designed for use in nonpersonal computer devices, including industrial controllers, cash registers, automated teller machines (ATMs), gateways, Internet Protocol (IP) telephones, server appliances, Windows-based thin clients, advanced consumer electronics, and specialized handheld devices.

Microsoft
1 Microsoft Way
Redmond, WA 98052-6399
425-882-8080
www.microsoft.com

Glossary

A listing of words and expressions related to Web services.

A

Active Server Pages—A Microsoft Web server technology. ASP allows the creation of dynamic, interactive users sessions. An ASP is a Web page that contains HTML and embedded programming code written in VBScript or Jscript.

Access Control—The protection of resources against unauthorized access. Access control is typically regulated according to a security policy, and access is permitted only by authorized system entities according to that policy.

Access Rights—A description of the type of authorized interactions a subject can have with a resource. Examples include read, write, execute, add, modify, and delete.

Account—The set of attributes that, together, define a user's access to a given service. Each service may define a unique set of attributes to define an account. An account defines user or system access to a resource or service.

Administrator—A person who maintains a Web services–based system.

ANSI X12—A protocol from the American National Standards Institute (ANSI) for electronic data interchange (EDI). ANSI X12 is the primary North American standard for defining EDI transactions.

Application Service Provider—An organization that hosts software applications on its own servers within its own facilities. Customers rent the use of the application and access it over the Internet.

Architecture—The software architecture of a program, or computing system, is the structure or structures of the system, which comprise software components, the externally visible properties of those components, and the relationships among them.

ASP—(see Application Service Provider).

ASP—(see Active Server Pages).

Authentication—The process of positively verifying the identity of a user, device, or other entity in a computer system, often as a prerequisite to allowing access to system resources.

Authorization—The process of determining, by evaluating applicable access control information, whether a subject is allowed to have specified types of access to a particular resource. Authorization typically takes place in the context of authentication. Once a subject is authenticated, it may be authorized to perform different types of access.

B

B2B—Business-to-business.

B2C—Business-to-consumer.

Binding—An association between an interface, a protocol, and a data format. A binding specifies the protocol and data format to be used in transmitting messages defined by the associated interface.

Browser—A software component that allows an end user to access a Web site. A browser provides a runtime environment for distributed application components on the client's device.

C

C++—An object-oriented version of C that is widely used to develop enterprise and commercial applications.

Client—A system entity that accesses a Web service; software that makes use of a Web Service.

Common Object Request Broker Architecture (CORBA)—A standard for communicating between distributed objects.

Confidentiality—Assurance that information will be kept secret, with access limited only to designated individuals.

CORBA—(see Common Object Request Broker Architecture).

COM—(see Component Object Model).

Component Object Model—A Microsoft component software architecture. Component Object Model defines a structure for building program routines (objects) that can be called up and executed in a Windows NT environment.

Customer Relationship Management (CRM)—An information system that is used to plan, schedule, and control the sales activities within an organization.

CRM (see Customer Relationship Management).

D

DNS—(see Domain Name System).

Domain Name System—The name resolution software that allows users to locate computers, or other resources, on the Internet by domain name.

E

ebXML—(see E-Business Extensible Markup Language).

E-Business Extensible Markup Language (ebXML)—An XML variant cosponsored by a United Nations standards agency and Oasis, a nonprofit organization. It was developed to provide a complete framework for XML-based B2B transactions. It has built-in security features for safeguarding confidential transactions.

EDI—(see Electronic Data Interchange).

EDIFACT—(see Electronic Data Interchange For Administration Commerce and Transport).

EJB—(see Enterprise JavaBeans).

Electronic Commerce—The conduct of various kinds of business transactions, covering trade, transport, finance, and related functions, electronically.

Electronic Data Interchange—The electronic communication of business transactions, including orders and invoices, between organizations.

Electronic Data Interchange For Administration Commerce and Transport—An ISO standard for electronic data interchange (EDI).

Enterprise JavaBeans—A software component in Sun's J2EE platform that provides a pure Java environment for developing and running distributed applications.

Enterprise Resource Planning—An integrated information system that serves several or all enterprise departments. ERP software typically consists of separate, interoperable modules.

ERP—(see Enterprise Resource Planning).

Extensible Markup Language (XML)—An open standard for describing data that is used for elements on a Web page and business-to-business documents. It has become the standard for defining data interchange formats on the Internet. It is similar to Hyper Text Markup Language (HTML) in that it uses tags to encode information. But, while HTML tells browsers how to display information, XML defines values for the information. Extensible Markup Language also lets users create their own tags.

F

File Transfer Protocol—A protocol used to transfer files over a TCP/IP network.

FTP—(see File Transfer Protocol).

H

Host—To run an application on an execution platform, which typically consists of hardware and software.

HTTP—(see Hyper Text Transfer Protocol).

Hyper Text Transfer Protocol—The communications protocol that is used to connect to servers on the Web.

I

IDL—(see Interface Definition Language).

Interface Definition Language—A language used to describe the interface to a particular routine or function. Objects in CORBA, for example, are defined by an IDL, which describes the services performed by the object and how information is to be passed to it.

Integrity—Assurance that information will not be accidentally, or maliciously, altered or destroyed.

International Organization for Standardization—A network of national standards institutes of some 140 countries. A central office in Geneva, Switzerland, coordinates the system and publishes finished standards.

ISO—(see International Organization for Standardization).

J

J2EE—(see Java 2 Platform, Enterprise Edition).

Java—An object-oriented programming language. Java is designed to generate applications that can run on all hardware platforms without modification.

JavaScript—A widely used scripting language that's extensively supported in Web browsers and other Web tools.

Java 2 Platform, Enterprise Edition (J2EE)—A Sun Microsystems technology that provides a component-based approach to the design, development, assembly, and deployment of enterprise applications. The J2EE platform offers a multitiered distributed application model, the ability to reuse components, integrated Extensible Markup Language (XML)–based data interchange, a unified security model, and flexible transaction control.

Jini—A Sun Microsystems Java-based distributed computing environment. With Jini (pronounced "gee-nee"), devices can be plugged into a network and to share-and-use services. As a result, any PDA or laptop to be plugged in the network would be able to instantly use printers and other resources.

JScript—Microsoft's version of JavaScript.

M

Message—The basic unit of communication between a Web service and a client.

Microsoft .NET—Microsoft .NET is a set of Microsoft software technologies for enabling software integration through the use of Web services.

N

.NET—(see Microsoft .NET).

Nonrepudiation—Method by which the sender of data is provided with proof of delivery, and the recipient is assured of the sender's identity, so that neither can later deny having processed the data.

O

Operation—A set of messages related to a single Web service action.

P

Port—An association between a binding and a network address, specified by a URI, that may be used to communicate with an instance of a service. A port indicates a specific location for accessing a service using a specific protocol and data format.

Provider—A business entity that sells access to, or use of, Web services.

Proxy Server—A computer process that relays a protocol between client and server computer systems, by appearing to the client to be the server and appearing to the server to be the client.

Pull—To actively request information from a system entity.

Push—To provide information to a system entity that didn't actively request it.

R

ROI—(See Return on Investment).

Repository—A database of information about applications software. A repository may include details on authorship, data elements, inputs, outputs, processes, and interrelationships.

Return on Investment—The measurement of how effectively an enterprise uses its capital. It is usually stated as a percentage over a specific time period. Calculating ROI involves two parts: knowing what to measure, and understanding how to translate the value of those measurements into actual dollars.

RosettaNet—A set of Internet-based standards, RosettaNet encompasses data dictionaries, an implementation framework, and business message schemas and process specifications for e-business standardization.

recML—An XML data standard that defines terms for recreation facilities (trails, campgrounds, etc.), activities (hiking, wildlife viewing, etc.), and transactions (reservations, fees, etc.).

S

Schema—(see XML schema).

Secure Sockets Layer—The Internet's most widely used security protocol. When an SSL session is launched, the server sends a public key to the Web browser. The browser then uses the key to send a randomly generated secret key back to the server to provide a secret key exchange for that session.

Security Policy—A set of rules and practices that specify, or regulate, how a system or organization provides security services to protect resources. Security policies are components of security architectures. Significant portions of security policies are implemented via security services, using security policy expressions.

Server—A computer located in a network that's shared by multiple users.

Service Attribute—Characteristics, or qualifiers, of a service. A service attribute describes details such as the type of encoding, a network address, a mailbox size, and so on.

Service Option—An available choice within an overall service. A service option is usually a custom choice provided by the service provider, as opposed to a service attribute, which is inherent to a service.

Service Provider—An organization that provides a particular type of network service.

Site—An informal term for an administrative domain in either a geographical or DNS name sense.

SOAP—(see Simple Object Access Protocol).

Simple Object Access Protocol—an XML-based protocol for exchanging information in a decentralized, distributed environment. It provides an envelope that defines a framework for describing what is in a message and how to process it, encoding rules for expressing application-defined data types, and a convention for representing remote procedure calls and responses.

SSL—(see Secure Sockets Layer).

System Entity—An active element of a computer or network system.

T

TCP/IP—(see Transmission Control Protocol/Internet Protocol).

Transmission Control Protocol/Internet Protocol—The UNIX standard that became the Internet's protocol, and has now become the global standard for data communications.

U

Uniform Resource Identifier—The addressing technology that identifies every file stored on the Internet.

UDDI—(see Universal Description, Discovery, and Integration).

UMI—(see Unified Modeling Language).

Unified Modeling Language—An object-oriented analysis and design language developed by the Object Management Group (OMG).

Universal Description, Discovery, and Integration—An XML-based specification for a registry of businesses and the Web services they offer. By providing the necessary translations, it enables software to automatically discover Web services and integrate with them.

URI—(see Uniform Resource Identifier).

V

Value-Added Network—A network operator that offers services beyond basic transmission functions, such as EDI support, protocol conversion, and automatic error correction.

VAN—(see Value-Added Network).

VBScript—(see Visual Basic Script).

Visual Basic—Microsoft's version of the BASIC programming language. Visual Basic offers specialized features for developing Windows applications.

Visual Basic Script—A Microsoft scripting language that's a subset of Visual Basic. VBScript is widely used on the Web for both client processing within a Web page and server-side processing in Active Server Pages (ASPs).

W

W3C—(see World Wide Web Consortium).

Web Services—Software that knows how to talk to other types of software over a network. A Web service can be nearly any type of application that has the ability to define to other applications what it does, and it can perform that action for authorized applications or parties.

Web Services Description Language—Lets developers expose the syntax of a Web service. Using an XML format, WSDL describes network services as a set of endpoints operating on messages containing either document- or procedure-oriented information. The operations and messages are described abstractly, and then are bound to a concrete network protocol and message format to define the endpoints.

Web Services Interoperability Organization—A consortium founded by Microsoft, IBM, BEA Systems, and Intel, the organization (www.ws-i.org) is dedicated to the development of Web services. Its goals are to provide guidance and education, to promote interoperability, and to ensure that Web services evolve and become widely used.

World Wide Web Consortium—A nonprofit organization that develops interoperable technologies (specifications, guidelines, software, and tools) that are designed to lead the Web to its full potential.

WSDL—(see Web Services Description Language).

WS-I—(see Web Services Interoperability Organization).

X

X12—(see ANSI X12).

XML Schema—XML Schemas express shared vocabularies and allow machines to carry out rules made by people. They provide a means for defining the structure, content, and semantics of XML documents.

XML—(see Extensible Markup Language).

Index